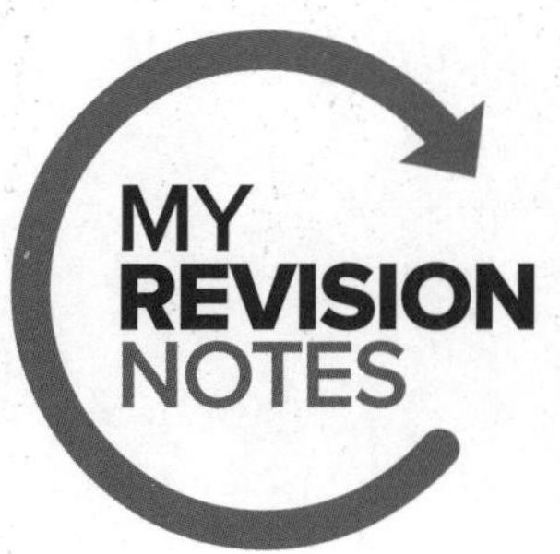

Pearson Ede

A-level

POLITICS: US POLITICS

SECOND EDITION

Anthony J. Bennett
Angela Mogridge

Orders: please contact Hachette UK Distribution, Hely Hutchinson Centre, Milton Road, Didcot, Oxfordshire, OX11 7HH. Telephone: +44 (0)1235 827827. Email education@hachette.co.uk Lines are open from 9 a.m. to 5 p.m., Monday to Friday. You can also order through our website: www.hoddereducation.co.uk

ISBN 978 1 3983 2551 7

First printed 2021

First published in 2021 by
Hodder Education,
An Hachette UK Company
Carmelite House
50 Victoria Embankment
London EC4Y 0DZ

www.hoddereducation.co.uk

Impression number 10 9 8 7 6 5 4 3 2 1

Year 2025 2024 2023 2022 2021

Cover photo: Tupungato – stock.adobe.com

Typeset in India by Aptara, Inc.

Printed in India

A catalogue record for this title is available from the British Library.

Get the most from this book

Everyone has to decide his or her own revision strategy, but it is essential to review your work, learn it and test your understanding. These Revision Notes will help you to do that in a planned way, topic by topic. Use this book as the cornerstone of your revision and do not hesitate to write in it — personalise your notes and check your progress by ticking off each section as you revise.

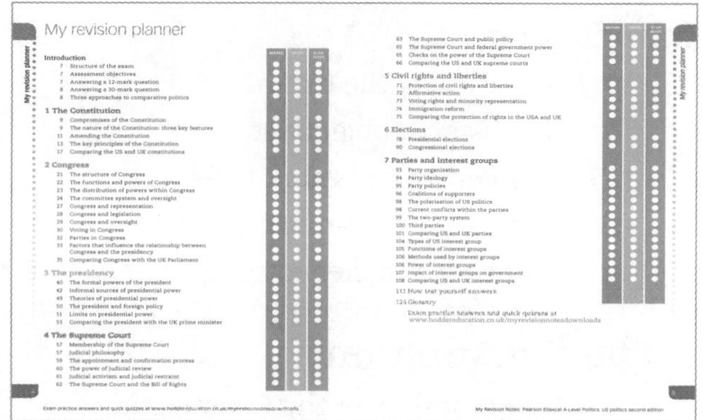

My revision planner

Introduction
- 7 Structure of the exam
- 7 Assessment objectives
- 7 Answering a 12-mark question
- 8 Answering a 30-mark question
- 8 Three approaches to comparative politics

1 The Constitution
- 9 Compromises of the Constitution
- 9 The nature of the Constitution: three key features
- 11 Amending the Constitution
- 13 The key principles of the Constitution
- 17 Comparing the US and UK constitutions

2 Congress
- 21 The structure of Congress
- 22 The functions and powers of Congress
- 23 The distribution of powers within Congress
- 24 The committee system and oversight
- 27 Congress and representation
- 28 Congress and legislation
- 29 Congress and oversight
- 30 Voting in Congress
- 32 Parties in Congress
- 33 Factors that influence the relationship between Congress and the presidency
- 35 Comparing Congress with the UK Parliament

3 The presidency
- 40 The formal powers of the president
- 42 Informal sources of presidential power
- 49 Theories of presidential power
- 50 The president and foreign policy
- 51 Limits on presidential power
- 53 Comparing the president with the UK prime minister

4 The Supreme Court
- 57 Membership of the Supreme Court
- 57 Judicial philosophy
- 59 The appointment and confirmation process
- 60 The power of judicial review
- 61 Judicial activism and judicial restraint
- 62 The Supreme Court and the Bill of Rights
- 63 The Supreme Court and public policy
- 65 The Supreme Court and federal government power
- 65 Checks on the power of the Supreme Court
- 66 Comparing the US and UK supreme courts

5 Civil rights and liberties
- 71 Protection of civil rights and liberties
- 72 Affirmative action
- 73 Voting rights and minority representation
- 74 Immigration reform
- 75 Comparing the protection of rights in the USA and UK

6 Elections
- 78 Presidential elections
- 90 Congressional elections

7 Parties and interest groups
- 93 Party organisation
- 94 Party ideology
- 95 Party policies
- 96 Coalitions of supporters
- 98 The polarisation of US politics
- 98 Current conflicts within the parties
- 99 The two-party system
- 100 Third parties
- 101 Comparing US and UK parties
- 104 Types of US interest group
- 105 Functions of interest groups
- 106 Methods used by interest groups
- 106 Power of interest groups
- 107 Impact of interest groups on government
- 108 Comparing US and UK interest groups

111 Now test yourself answers

124 Glossary

Exam practice answers and quick quizzes at www.hoddereducation.co.uk/myrevisionnotesdownloads

My Revision Notes: Pearson Edexcel A-Level Politics: US politics second edition

Tick to track your progress 

Use the revision planner on pages 4 and 5 to plan your revision, topic by topic. Tick each box when you have:

- revised and understood a topic
- tested yourself
- practised the exam questions and gone online to check your answers and complete the quick quizzes

You can also keep track of your revision by ticking off each topic heading in the book. You may find it helpful to add your own notes as you work through each topic.

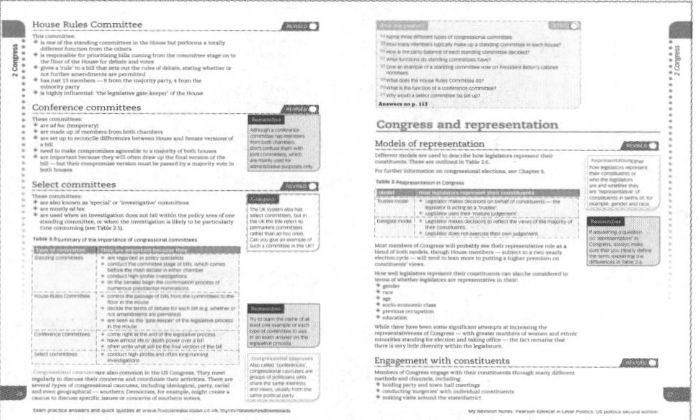

House Rules Committee

This committee:
- is one of the standing committees in the House but performs a totally different function from the others
- is responsible for prioritising bills coming from the committee stage on to the floor of the House for debate and votes
- gives a 'rule' to a bill that sets out the rules of debate, stating whether or not further amendments are permitted
- has just 13 members — 9 from the majority party, 4 from the minority party
- is highly influential: 'the legislative gate-keeper' of the House

Conference committees

These committees:
- are ad hoc (temporary)
- are made up of members from both chambers
- are set up to reconcile differences between House and Senate versions of a bill
- need to make compromises agreeable to a majority of both houses
- are important because they will often draw up the final version of the bill — but their compromise version must be passed by a majority vote in both houses

Although a conference committee has members from both chambers, don't confuse them with joint committees, which are mainly used for administrative purposes only.

Select committees

These committees:
- are also known as 'special' or 'investigative' committees
- are mostly ad hoc
- are used when an investigation does not fall within the policy area of one standing committee, or when the investigation is likely to be particularly time consuming (see Table 2.5).

The UK system also has select committees, but in the UK the title refers to permanent committees rather than ad hoc ones. Can you give an example of such a committee in the UK?

Try to learn the name of at least one example of each type of committee to use in an exam answer on the legislative process

Congressional caucuses are also common in the US Congress. They meet regularly to discuss their concerns and coordinate their activities. There are several types of congressional caucuses, including ideological, party, racial and even geographical — southern Democrats, for example, might create a caucus to discuss specific issues or concerns of southern voters.

Congressional caucuses Also called 'conferences', congressional caucuses are groups of politicians who share the same interests and views, usually from the same political party.

Answers on p. 113

Congress and representation

Models of representation

Different models are used to describe how legislators represent their constituents. These are outlined in Table 2.6.

For further information on congressional elections, see Chapter 6.

Most members of Congress will probably see their representative role as a blend of both models, though House members — subject to a two-yearly election cycle — will tend to lean more to putting a higher premium on constituents' views.

How well legislators represent their constituents can also be considered in terms of whether legislators are representative in their:
- gender
- race
- age
- socio-economic class
- previous occupation
- education

While there have been some significant attempts at increasing the representativeness of Congress — with greater numbers of women and ethnic minorities standing for election and taking office — the fact remains that there is very little diversity within the legislature.

Engagement with constituents

Members of Congress engage with their constituents through many different methods and channels, including:
- holding party and town hall meetings
- conducting 'surgeries' with individual constituents
- making visits around the state/district

My Revision Notes: Pearson Edexcel A-Level Politics: US politics second edition

Features to help you succeed

Now test yourself

These short, knowledge-based questions provide the first step in testing your learning. Answers are at the back of the book.

Definitions and key words

Clear, concise definitions of essential key terms are provided where they first appear.

Making links

This feature identifies specific connections between topics and tells you how revising these will aid your exam answers.

Exam skills

These summaries highlight how the specific skills identified or applicable in a chapter can be applied to your exam answers.

Compare

This feature shows you how to make comparisons with UK content.

Summaries

The summaries provide a quick-check bullet list for each topic.

Revision activities

These activities will help you to understand each topic in an interactive way.

Exam practice

Practice exam questions are provided for each topic. Use them to consolidate your revision and practise your exam skills.

Online

Go online to check your answers to the exam questions and try out the extra quick quizzes at **www.hoddereducation.co.uk/myrevisionnotesdownloads**

My revision planner

Exam practice answers and quick quizzes at
www.hoddereducation.co.uk/myrevisionnotesdownloads

Countdown to my exams

6–8 weeks to go

- Start by looking at the specification — make sure you know exactly what material you need to revise and the style of the examination. Use the revision planner on pages 4 and 5 to familiarise yourself with the topics.
- Organise your notes, making sure you have covered everything on the specification. The revision planner will help you to group your notes into topics.
- Work out a realistic revision plan that will allow you time for relaxation. Set aside days and times for all the subjects that you need to study, and stick to your timetable.
- Set yourself sensible targets. Break your revision down into focused sessions of around 40 minutes, divided by breaks. These Revision Notes organise the basic facts into short, memorable sections to make revising easier.

REVISED

4–6 weeks to go

- Read through the relevant sections of this book and refer to the reminders, key terms and summaries. Tick off the topics as you feel confident about them. Highlight those topics you find difficult and look at them again in detail.
- Test your understanding of each topic by working through the 'Now test yourself' questions in the book. Look up the answers at the back of the book.
- Make a note of any problem areas as you revise, and ask your teacher to go over these in class.
- Look at past papers. They are one of the best ways to revise and practise your exam skills. Write or prepare planned answers to the exam practice questions provided in this book. Check your answers online and try out the extra quick quizzes at **www.hoddereducation.co.uk/myrevisionnotesdownloads**
- Try using different revision methods as you work through the sections. For example, you can make notes using concept maps, spider diagrams or flash cards.
- Track your progress using the revision planner and give yourself a reward when you have achieved your target.

REVISED

One week to go

- Try to fit in at least one more timed practice of an entire past paper and seek feedback from your teacher, comparing your work closely with the mark scheme.
- Check the revision planner to make sure you haven't missed out any topics. Brush up on any areas of difficulty by talking them over with a friend or getting help from your teacher.
- Attend any revision classes put on by your teacher. Remember, your teacher is an expert at preparing people for examinations.

REVISED 

The day before the examination

- Flick through these Revision Notes for useful reminders, key terms and summaries.
- Check the time and place of your examination.
- Make sure you have everything you need — extra pens and pencils, tissues, a watch, bottled water, sweets.
- Allow some time to relax and have an early night to ensure you are fresh and alert for the examination.

REVISED

My exams

Paper 1: UK Politics

Date: ....

Time: ....

Location: ....

Paper 2: UK Government

Date: ....

Time: ....

Location: ....

Paper 3: Comparative Politics

Date: ....

Time: ....

Location: ....

Introduction

Structure of the exam

US politics is examined in the Component 3A: Comparative Politics exam paper. It is a 2-hour exam which is worth 84 marks, a third of the total marks for A-level Politics.

In Section A, you need to answer ONE 12-mark question from a choice of two. This section tests AO1 and AO2 (see below) and the question will require you to 'Examine...' something. This will be a comparative question.

Section B is similar but there is only ONE compulsory question, again examining AO1 and AO2. This question will require you to 'Analyse...' something.

Section C is focused on US politics alone and requires you to write TWO 30-mark essay answers. This examines AO1, AO2 and AO3. You will choose TWO questions from a choice of three. These questions will require you to 'Evaluate...' something.

Assessment objectives

The three assessment objectives (AOs) require you to:

AO1 Demonstrate knowledge and understanding of political concepts, issues and theories.
AO2 Analyse aspects of political concepts, issues and theories.
AO3 Evaluate aspects of politics and make substantiated judgements and conclusions.

Remember

If the exam question asks you to **'Examine'** something, you need to consider it in detail and identify the similarities and differences with something else. So, for example, if the question was 'Examine the ways in which the US Senate and the UK House of Lords differ', you would need to identify and then consider in detail all of the differences between the two legislative chambers.

Answering a 12-mark question

You have 2 hours to complete the whole exam, so should spend around 20 minutes answering each 12-mark question. In order to gain high marks, you should aim to examine and analyse around five or six different points — each of which will need elaborating on.

The Section B 12-mark question explicitly states that you need to make reference to at least one comparative theory — this means that when discussing similarities and differences, you must mention the comparative theory that is most relevant to your point. See the discussion on page 8 for more information.

Remember

If you are asked to **'Analyse'** something, you need to examine, explain and interpret in detail an aspect of politics. If the question was, for example, 'Analyse the differences between the ways in which rights are protected in the USA and the UK', you would need to do more than identify the differences — you would need to elaborate on each difference and assess its importance or its relevance.

Answering a 30-mark question

A 30-mark question requires you to write an essay. You have to answer TWO of these questions in Section C, and should spend 40 minutes on **each** question. You are expected to provide a balanced argument and then reach a substantiated judgement in your conclusion. You should discuss at least four points on either side of the argument and then, in your conclusion, come down on one side or the other. Remember that you should not be writing phrases such as 'I believe...' or 'in my opinion...' — use more academic phrases such as 'on balance...', 'as has been shown...', or 'in light of what has been discussed...'.

Remember

If the exam question asks you to **'Evaluate'** something, you need to consider the arguments and come to a conclusion about their importance or success. So, if you were asked to 'Evaluate the extent to which Congress is an effective legislative body', you would need to consider all the arguments that Congress **is** effective and all that arguments that it **isn't** effective and then, in light of the arguments for and against, make a decision about whether Congress is or isn't effective.

Remember

If an exam question asks you to '**Evaluate the extent** to which...' it requires you to weigh up both sides of an argument or an issue and reach a judgement one way or another. So, if the question was 'Evaluate the extent to which the Supreme Court has quasi-legislative powers', you would need to discuss the arguments that the Supreme Court **does** have quasi-legislative powers **and** the arguments that the Supreme Court **does not** have quasi-legislative powers. You would then need to reach a conclusion based on the arguments and decide whether the evidence in favour of the Court having these powers outweighs the arguments against.

Three approaches to comparative politics

For A-Level Politics you are required to look at three different approaches to explaining similarities and differences between the political systems of different countries. In your Section B 12-mark answer, you must refer to at least one of these approaches.

Rational theory

This focuses on the individual within a political system and assumes that they will act rationally in a self-interested way. You could refer to rational theory when discussing the fact that prime ministers might use their popularity with the electorate to persuade Parliament to pass legislation.

Cultural theory

This focuses on groups within the political system and how these groups shape ideas and determine actions. You could refer to cultural theory when comparing the actions of US and UK interest groups or when comparing the policies of US and UK political parties.

Structural theory

This focuses on the institutions within the political system and how outcomes are determined by processes within these institutions. You might refer to structural theory when comparing the checks and balances that the US and UK legislatures bring to bear on the executive.

1 The Constitution

Compromises of the Constitution

The form of government

REVISED

Under British control, the colonies had been ruled by a unitary form of government, in which political power rests with one central/national government (of Great Britain in this case).

From 1781, they had then been ruled under a confederal form of government — one in which virtually all political power rests with the individual states and little with the central/national government.

The compromise was to devise a new form of government — a federal form of government, one in which some political power rests with the national (known as the federal) government, but other, equally important, powers rest with the state governments.

Remember

Notice 'equally important' — it's crucial to include that phrase so as not to give the impression that the state governments' powers are trivial.

Representation of the states

- Large-population states wanted representation in Congress to be proportional to population: the bigger the population of a state, the more representatives it would have in Congress.
- Small-population states wanted equal representation.
- The compromise was to have Congress made up of two houses — the House of Representatives and the Senate.
- In the House of Representatives, there would be representation proportional to population.
- In the Senate, there would be equal representation for all states, regardless of population.

Remember

Don't use the phrase 'proportional representation' — it isn't!

Remember

To save yourself time in the exam, use the term 'House' (with a capital H) to refer to the House of Representatives.

Choosing the president

There were many different suggestions about how to choose the president.

- Some thought the president should be appointed.
- Others thought the president should be directly elected by the people.
- The compromise was to have the president indirectly elected by an Electoral College (see Chapter 6).

Now test yourself

TESTED

1 What was the disagreement between large-population states and small-population states with reference to representation?

2 Give three examples of compromises in the Constitution.

Answers on p. 111

The nature of the Constitution: three key features

The Constitution has three key features:

1 It is codified.
2 Some of it is specific but some of it is vague.
3 Its provisions are entrenched.

Constitution A set of political principles by which a country or organisation is governed.

Codification The process of arranging rules or processes in written format.

A codified constitution

REVISED

Some constitutions, like that for the UK, are uncodified — they are not collected together in one document — while others, such as that of the USA, are codified. This means there is one document called the Constitution.

But it's worth remembering that these two terms are not exclusive to one another, and they are not the same as 'written' and 'unwritten' constitutions. Codified constitutions may not include all constitutional provisions. Written constitutions may have some elements that are unwritten.

Codified constitution A constitution that consists of a full and authoritative set of rules written down in a single document.

The new Constitution was made up of seven Articles, the first three of which explained how the three branches of the federal (national) government — Congress, the president and the Supreme Court — would work and what powers they would have (see Table 1.1).

Table 1.1 Summary of Articles I, II and III of the Constitution

Article I	Established Congress as the national legislature (law-making body) and defined its membership, method of election and powers
Article II	Established the president as chief executive and defined their method of election and powers
Article III	Established the US Supreme Court and set out its membership, method of appointment and powers

This leads us to the second of the Constitution's three key features — that some of it is specific and some of it is vague.

A blend of specificity and vagueness

REVISED

Some of the powers the Constitution gives, especially to Congress, are very specific:

- The power 'to collect taxes' (Article I)
- The power 'to coin money' (Article I)

But others are quite vague:

- The power of Congress 'to provide for the common defence and general welfare of the United States' (Article I)
- The power of Congress 'to make all laws which shall be necessary and proper for carrying into execution the foregoing powers' (Article I)

There is also the issue of whether certain powers belong only to the federal government, only to the state governments, or to both the federal and state governments. Table 1.2 explains these different types of power.

Enumerated powers Powers given to the federal government by the US Constitution.

Table 1.2 Summary of different types of power in the Constitution

Enumerated (or delegated) powers	Powers delegated to the federal government — generally those enumerated in the first three Articles of the Constitution	For example: the vice president is also president of the Senate and has the casting vote in the event of a tied vote.
Implied powers	Powers possessed by the federal government by inference from those powers delegated to it in the Constitution	For example: the power to draft people into the armed forces may be implied by Congress's enumerated power to raise an army and navy.
Reserved powers	Powers not delegated to the federal government, or prohibited to it by the Constitution — these are 'reserved' to the states or to the people	For example: marriage and divorce laws differ between states.
Concurrent powers	Powers possessed by both the federal and state governments	For example: highway management and maintenance. The federal government is responsible for US highways and the interstate system, while individual states manage intrastate highways.

Entrenched provisions

REVISED

Entrenchment is written into the Constitution by the complicated and demanding process for amending it.

Entrenchment The application of extra legal safeguards to a constitutional provision to make it more difficult to amend or abolish.

Now test yourself

TESTED

3 What are the three key features of the Constitution?
4 What is a codified constitution?
5 What do the first three Articles of the Constitution deal with?
6 Give an example of the vagueness of the Constitution.
7 What is the difference between enumerated powers and implied powers?
8 What is the difference between reserved powers and concurrent powers?
9 What does 'entrenchment' mean?

Answers on p. 111

Amending the Constitution

The various methods for amending the Constitution are set out in Table 1.3.

Table 1.3 The process for amending the Constitution

	Proposed by	Ratified by	How often used?
1	Two-thirds of the House and the Senate	Three-quarters of the state legislatures (38)	26 times
2	Two-thirds of the House and the Senate	**Ratifying** conventions in three-quarters of the states	Once (Twenty-First Amendment)
3	Legislatures in two-thirds of the states calling for a national constitutional convention	Three-quarters of the state legislatures	Never
4	Legislatures in two-thirds of the states calling for a national constitutional convention	Ratifying conventions in three-quarters of the states	Never

Ratify To sign and give official consent to a change or amendment.

Supermajority Where approval is required by a two-thirds majority of Congress.

Remember

The president has no formal role in passing constitutional amendments. Having been agreed by both houses of Congress, they are not subject to presidential approval and neither can the president veto them.

As Table 1.3 shows, all successful attempts at amending the Constitution have been by amendments being:

+ proposed by two-thirds majorities of both houses of Congress
+ ratified by three-quarters (now 38) of the state legislatures

Advantages and disadvantages of the amendment process are outlined in Table 1.4.

Table 1.4 Advantages and disadvantages of the amendment process

Advantages of the amendment process	Disadvantages of the amendment process
+ **Supermajorities** ensure against a small majority being able to impose its will on a large minority. + The lengthy and complicated process makes it less likely that the Constitution will be amended on a merely temporary issue. + It ensures that both the federal and state governments must favour a proposal. + It gives a magnified voice to the smaller-population states (through the Senate's role and the requirement for agreement of three-quarters of state legislatures). + The provision for a constitutional convention called by the states prevents Congress from being able to veto an amendment without the consent of the states.	+ It makes it overly difficult for the Constitution to be amended, thereby perpetuating what some see as outdated provisions (e.g. the Electoral College). + It makes possible the thwarting of the will of the majority by a small and possibly unrepresentative minority. + The lengthy and complicated process nonetheless allowed the Prohibition amendment to be passed (1918), banning the manufacture, sale and transportation of alcohol. + The difficulty of formal amendment enhances the power of the (unelected) Supreme Court to make interpretative amendments. + The voice of small-population states is overly represented.

Remember

In the exam you may be asked to come to a conclusion about how effective the amendment process is. Make sure you have a bank of examples to use to illustrate your answer (e.g. names of some small-population states, some amendments that have been passed and some that have been proposed but not passed).

The Bill of Rights and later amendments

REVISED

Of the 27 amendments to the Constitution, the first ten were proposed together by Congress in September 1789 and are collectively known as the Bill of Rights. These include:

- Freedom of religion, speech, the press and assembly (First Amendment)
- Right to keep and bear arms (Second Amendment)
- Rights of accused persons (Fifth Amendment)
- Prohibition of cruel and unusual punishments (Eighth Amendment)
- Undelegated powers reserved to the states or to the people (Tenth Amendment)

Amendments added later include:

- Prohibition of slavery (Thirteenth Amendment, 1865)
- Federal government granted power to impose income tax (Sixteenth Amendment, 1913)
- Direct election of the Senate (Seventeenth Amendment, 1913)
- Two-term limit for the president (Twenty-Second Amendment, 1951)
- Presidential succession and disability procedures (Twenty-Fifth Amendment, 1967)
- Voting age lowered to 18 (Twenty-Sixth Amendment, 1971).

Making links

The ten amendments that make up the Bill of Rights are extremely important to American citizens and are often quoted when a citizen has a grievance. The Second Amendment, for example, is often quoted as evidence of the right to bear arms in the USA. Accused persons will often quote the Fifth Amendment — the right to remain silent when being questioned by the police. Interest groups will reference the Bill of Rights wherever possible to reinforce their campaigns for change or the protection of the rights of their members (see Chapter 7).

Remember

Note that a question about amending the US Constitution could require quite a substantial discussion about the Supreme Court's power of judicial review.

There have been only 27 successful attempts to amend the Constitution and only 15 since 1805. That is pretty infrequent. So why has the Constitution been so rarely amended? Reasons include the following:

- The Founding Fathers created a deliberately difficult process.
- The Constitution is, in parts, deliberately vague and has therefore evolved without the need for formal amendment.
- The Supreme Court has the power of judicial review (see Chapter 4).
- Americans have become cautious about tampering with the Constitution.

Interpretative amendment The ability of the Supreme Court to interpret the Constitution and, in effect, change the meaning of words within it.

Debate

Does the US Constitution still work? Does it ensure democracy in the USA and curtail the power of the executive?

Yes	No
+ Federalism has proved to be an excellent compromise between strong national government and state government diversity. + The text has proved very adaptable to changes in US society. + The demanding amendment process has usually prevented frequent and ill-conceived proposals for amendment. + Rights and liberties of Americans have been protected. + The Supreme Court's power of judicial review has made it even more adaptable through '**interpretative amendment**'.	+ The amendment process is too difficult, thereby making it well-nigh impossible to amend parts no longer applicable or to add parts that a majority desires. + Power of judicial review gives the Supreme Court too much power to 'amend' its meaning. + The Constitution is too negative, giving too much power to those who oppose change. + Some parts make little sense in today's society (e.g. the Electoral College). + Some parts don't work as the framers would have envisaged (e.g. war-making powers).

Now test yourself TESTED

10 How can constitutional amendments be proposed?
11 How can constitutional amendments be ratified?
12 Give three advantages and three disadvantages of the amendment process.
13 What are the first ten amendments to the Constitution called?
14 Give two examples of subsequent constitutional amendments.
15 Give two reasons why the Constitution has been amended so rarely.

Answers on p. 111

Remember

You should make a judgement for yourself on whether the Constitution continues to work or whether it needs changing, as you could be asked a question about this in the exam. Make sure you have examples to hand to illustrate your argument (e.g. aspects of the modern world which are not adequately accommodated in the Constitution, or events which have shown that the Constitution is still relevant).

The key principles of the Constitution

The Constitution is based on five key principles:

1 Separation of powers
2 Checks and balances
3 Federalism
4 Bipartisanship
5 Limited government

Separation of powers

REVISED 

To understand the principle of the separation of powers, you need to realise the following:

- The federal government is made up of three separate branches:
  - The legislature (Congress), which makes the laws.

Remember

Be careful not to confuse the word 'legislature' (a noun, as in 'the legislature') with the word 'legislative' (an adjective, as in 'the legislative process').

  - The executive (headed by the president), which carries out (executes) the laws.
  - The judiciary (headed by the Supreme Court), which enforces and interprets the laws.
- No one can belong to more than one of these branches at the same time — this is often referred to as 'the separation of powers'.
- The term is somewhat misleading as it's not the 'powers' that are separate but the institutions themselves.
- Therefore the Constitution created a governmental system made up of **'separated institutions, sharing powers'**.

This sharing of powers is what the second of the Constitution's key principles — checks and balances — is about.

Compare

The UK Constitution does not provide for a similar separation of powers principle. It is possible to be a member of more than one branch of government in the UK. Give two examples of where this has happened in recent governments.

Separation of powers A theory of government whereby political power is distributed among the legislature, the executive and the judiciary, each acting both independently and interdependently.

Checks and balances A system of government that gives each branch — legislative, executive and judicial — the means partially to control the power exercised by the other branches.

Remember

The four-word phrase 'separated institutions, sharing powers' is well worth committing to memory.

Checks and balances

REVISED

Because the Constitution creates a system of separate institutions that share powers, each institution can check the powers of the others. The major checks possessed by each branch are set out in Table 1.5, along with some recent examples.

Table 1.5 Examples of major checks and balances

Check by the president on Congress	
Veto a bill	Iran War Powers Resolution (Trump, 2020)
Checks by the president on the federal courts	
Nominate judges	Brett Kavanaugh (Trump, 2018)
Pardon	Of Bernard Kerik, former New York City police commissioner (Trump, 2020)
Commutation of sentences	Of Roger Stone, political consultant and Trump confidant (Trump, 2020)
Checks by Congress on the president	
Amend/delay/reject legislative proposals	American Health Care Act (2017) — Trump's attempt to repeal and replace 'Obamacare'
Override veto	National Defense Authorization Act for 2021 (2020)
Refuse to approve appointments*	John Tower as secretary of defense (1989)
Refuse to ratify treaties*	Convention on the Rights of Persons with Disabilities (2012)
Impeachment and trial	Of President Donald Trump (2019–20 and 2021)
Checks by Congress on the federal courts	
Propose constitutional amendments	Proposed Federal Marriage Amendment (2015)
Refuse to approve appointments*	Merrick Garland to the Supreme Court (2016)
Check by the federal courts on Congress	
Declare law unconstitutional	Defense of Marriage Act (1996) in 2013
Check by the federal courts on the president	
Declare actions unconstitutional	Declared unconstitutional President Trump's claim that he did not have to comply with a subpoena from a New York district attorney seeking information on Trump's personal and business financial dealings (2020)

* Senate only.

Impeachment A formal accusation of serious wrongdoing or misconduct of a serving federal official by a simple majority vote of the House of Representatives.

Making links

These checks and balances link to the power and effectiveness of the different institutions. For example, Congress has 'the power of the purse' and must agree to the money needed by the president for the president's policies. A Congress that is dominated by the opposing party to the president can wield a significant amount of power over the ability of the president to get things done (see Chapter 2).

Remember

Always try to have examples that are as up to date as possible in your answers — avoid using examples that are unnecessarily dated.

Compare

In the UK, separation of powers does not exist, but there is a system of checks and balances. What powers does the UK Parliament have to check a prime minister's power?

Federalism

REVISED

The third key principle of the Constitution is **federalism**.

Nowhere is the word 'federal' or 'federalism' mentioned in the Constitution. It was written into the document in:

- the enumerated powers of the federal government
- the implied powers of the federal government
- the concurrent powers of the federal and state governments
- the Tenth Amendment

Federalism A theory of government by which political power is divided between a national government and state governments, each having their own areas of substantive jurisdiction.

Compare

The UK is an example of a unitary system rather than a federalist state. A significant degree of devolution has, however, taken place in the UK in recent decades. Give two similarities and two differences between devolution and federalism.

Federalism under Barack Obama

Democrat president Barack Obama (2009–17) focused on domestic policy in order to pursue his 'change' agenda. The Obama years saw an increase in federal government activity in such programmes as:

- an economic stimulus package (2009)
- the re-authorisation of the State Children's Health Insurance Program (S-CHIP) (2009)
- the expansion of Medicaid (health insurance programme for the poor)
- 'Obamacare' — Obama's flagship reform of the US healthcare system (2010)

Federalism under Donald Trump

Republican presidents have traditionally sought to shrink the size and scope of the federal government. Although President Trump (2017–21) generally agreed with that policy, there were times when he attempted to make the states subservient to the federal government, but mostly in ways that specifically increased the power of the president, such as:

- trying to end state lockdowns during the Covid-19 pandemic
- policies towards illegal immigrants and 'sanctuary cities'
- use of the national guard and federal troops during the Black Lives Matter protests of May/June 2020

Consequences of federalism

Federalism has consequences throughout US government and politics:

- Legal consequences — there is variation in state laws on such matters as the age at which people can marry or drive a car or have to attend school. Laws on the death penalty vary. There are federal and state courts.
- Policy consequences — states can act as policy laboratories, experimenting with new solutions to old problems. There is great variation between the states on such policies as healthcare provision, immigration, affirmative action and environmental protection.
- Consequences for elections — all elections are state-based and run under state law.
- Consequences for political parties — political parties in the USA are essentially decentralised, state-based parties.
- Economic consequences — huge federal grants going to the states, as well as the complexity of the tax system because, for example, income tax is levied by both federal and some state governments.
- Regionalism — the regions of the South, the Midwest, the Northeast and the West have distinct cultures as well as racial, religious and ideological differences.

Bipartisanship

REVISED

The Constitution makes no mention of political parties, but the separation of powers and the corresponding checks and balances between the three branches of the federal government — especially those between the legislature and the executive — mean that parties must cooperate. The framers of the Constitution hoped to encourage a spirit of bipartisanship and compromise between the president and Congress. Laws would be passed, treaties ratified, appointments confirmed and budgets fixed only when both parties worked together.

Bipartisanship Agreement or cooperation between two different political parties that usually oppose each other.

Limited government

REVISED

The final key principle of the Constitution is limited government. The system of checks and balances, in addition to the separation of powers, places a firm limit on the powers of the executive and restricts its actions.

Limited government A government prevented from being all-powerful by the limits provided by the Constitution.

Now test yourself

TESTED

16 What are the five key principles of the Constitution?

17 Define the doctrine of the separation of powers.

18 Complete this quotation: 'The Constitution created a governmental system made up of separated __________ sharing __________.'

19 Give an example of each of the six sets of checks between the three branches of the federal government.

20 Give a definition of federalism.

21 How was federalism written into the Constitution?

22 Give two examples of the ways in which the size and scope of the federal government expanded under (a) Barack Obama and (b) Donald Trump.

23 Give three examples of the consequences of federalism.

Answers on pp. 111–12

Debate

Is the USA still a federal nation?

Yes	No
+ All citizens pay federal income tax and the states depend on financial support from the federal government. + Healthcare provision is heavily dependent on federal funding, with the majority of states providing Medicaid. + The federal government has mandated parts of education policy. + The Homeland Security department coordinates and controls responses to threats to the nation (e.g. terrorist threats and natural disasters). + States depend on the federal government during national crises. The Federal Emergency Management Agency exists because the individual states cannot do what federal government can do. + The Supreme Court has made rulings in favour of the federal government over the states.	+ Laws vary significantly across states, including the legality of the death penalty, state taxes and the legal status of marijuana. + States control the provision of medical insurance. + Electoral practices vary significantly from state to state. + Some states use sanctuary cities to prohibit local law officers from helping federal immigration officials. + During national crises or national disasters such as Covid-19, state governors act in the best interests of their state. + The Supreme Court has made rulings in favour of a state over the federal government, e.g. *Texas* v *United States* (2016).

Comparing the US and UK constitutions

The origins of the two constitutions

REVISED

The differences between the constitutions of the USA and the UK largely reflect the different cultures of these two countries. This is where you can use the cultural approach to compare the constitutions. You can also use the rational approach given that the Founding Fathers conceived and wrote the US Constitution in response to their experiences during British rule — it was in their rational interests to lay out the 'rules' clearly to ensure limited government. Table 1.6 shows the different factors that shaped each constitution.

Table 1.6 Factors that shaped the US and UK constitutions

Factors that shaped the US Constitution	Factors that shaped the UK Constitution
✚ Liberty ✚ Individualism ✚ Equality ✚ Representative government ✚ Limited government ✚ States' rights ✚ Gun ownership ✚ Fear of state-organised religion	✚ An autocratic monarchy ✚ The hereditary principle ✚ The power of a landed aristocracy ✚ An established church ✚ A deferential working class ✚ A lack of social mobility

The nature of the two constitutions

REVISED

The two constitutions are different not only in origin but also in nature. They are structurally very different. The US Constitution is codified, yet it makes no mention at all of such important matters as:

- primary elections
- congressional committees
- the president's cabinet
- the Executive Office of the President
- the Supreme Court's power of judicial review

Some things that to begin with were merely conventions — such as a two-term limit for the president — over time have become formalised in the codified document.

The UK Constitution is uncodified, but much of it is written down in, for example:

- Acts of Parliament
- common law
- the works of Erskine May and Walter Bagehot

This is an ideal place to use the structural approach to comparative politics — you are clearly comparing the different elements, institutions and structures of the two constitutions.

Other important differences between the two constitutions are as follows:

- The powers, requirements and rights in the US Constitution are entrenched, whereas those in the UK Constitution are not.
- The US Constitution allows for much more popular and democratic participation than does the UK Constitution.
- The US Constitution establishes a separation of powers, whereas the UK Constitution establishes more in the way of fused powers, especially between the executive and the legislature.
- Checks and balances are more significant in the US Constitution than in the UK Constitution.
- The US Constitution enshrines the principle of federalism, whereas the UK Constitution enshrines the principle of devolution.

Table 1.7 summarises the main characteristics of the two constitutions and Table 1.8 compares UK devolution with federalism in the USA.

Table 1.7 Summary of comparisons between the US and UK constitutions

US Constitution	UK Constitution
Codified	Uncodified
Some (unwritten) conventions	Much is written
Entrenched	No entrenchment
More direct democratic participation	Emphasis on representative democracy
Separation of powers	Fusion of powers
Checks and balances	Fewer checks on power
Federalism	Devolution

Table 1.8 Comparing UK devolution with US federalism

Similarities between devolution and federalism	Differences between devolution and federalism
+ Both federalism and devolution involve a transfer of power from a central government to a regional government. Within the terms of the agreement, the regional government has the power to make laws and policies that may differ from those in other regions.	+ Federalism tends to be more rigid as it is defined by the Constitution and can only be changed by agreement between the federal government and the states. Devolution could be changed or removed much more easily through a simple law change. + With devolution, the central government maintains overall power. Having delegated some of its powers to regional governments, it remains more powerful than any devolved assemblies. With federalism, power is shared between the federal government and the states: the two are equally powerful; they just have different powers. + In a federal system all states have the same powers, whereas in a devolved system different regional assemblies can have different powers. For example, the Scottish Parliament has tax-raising powers while the Welsh Assembly does not. + Under devolution a regional assembly can be suspended on the say-so of the central government — this has happened, for example, with the Northern Ireland Assembly. Federalism does not allow this significant power to the federal government.

Now test yourself

24 Give three of the cultural factors that were important in the USA in the late eighteenth century that helped shape the US Constitution.

25 Give three of the cultural factors that helped shape the UK Constitution.

26 Give three aspects of US government and politics not mentioned in the Constitution.

27 Name three places where one can find written parts of the UK Constitution.

28 Name three important differences in the nature of the US and UK constitutions.

Answers on p. 112

Remember

Don't labour the point of written versus unwritten constitutions — the UK Constitution has many written parts despite its being considered by some as an unwritten constitution. It is more helpful to discuss codified and uncodified constitutions.

Using comparative approaches when comparing the US and UK constitutions

REVISED

Table 1.9 shows how the three comparative approaches can be used when comparing the constitutions of the USA and UK.

Table 1.9 Comparative approaches to comparing the US and UK constitutions

Topic	Rational approach	Cultural approach	Structural approach
Origins	The US Constitution is based on the values of rationality and individualism.	The US Constitution was written from a fear of an over-powerful ruler or state and a desire for limited government. The UK Constitution evolved over centuries and has been shaped by a culture dominated by the monarchy, an established church and an aristocracy.	The US Constitution was written at the beginning of the establishment of the US political system and remains a fundamental part of the process.
Codified/ uncodified		The US Constitution was written from a fear of an over-powerful ruler or state and a desire for limited government. The UK Constitution evolved over centuries and has been shaped by a culture dominated by the monarchy, an established church and an aristocracy.	Discussion of how the US Constitution is codified and its UK counterpart is uncodified — one written from scratch, the other evolving over time.
Entrenchment			The US constitution is entrenched and thus needs to go through a lengthy and difficult amendment process in order to change; the UK Constitution is not entrenched and is thus easy to change.
Separation/ fusion of powers			The US Constitution establishes a system of separated powers, whereas the UK Constitution allows more fusion of powers.
Checks and balances			Both the USA and the UK have a system of checks and balances but only the USA has these protected by the Constitution.
Federalism/ devolution			The US Constitution establishes the principle of federalism and the associated powers and roles of state and central government. The UK Constitution was flexible enough to allow for devolution in the 1990s.

Summary

You should now have an understanding of:

- ✚ why the US Constitution came to be written in its original form
- ✚ the significance of the process for constitutional amendment
- ✚ the link between separation of powers and checks and balances
- ✚ the way federalism works in the USA
- ✚ the similarities and differences between the US and UK constitutions and some of the reasons behind the differences
- ✚ the extent to which rational, structural and cultural comparative approaches can be used to account for these similarities and differences

Exam practice

Section A (comparative)

1 Examine the extent to which the US and UK constitutions are written and unwritten. [12]

2 Examine the provision of decentralisation in the US and UK constitutions. [12]

3 Examine the differences between devolution in the UK and federalism in the USA. [12]

4 Examine the similarities and differences between the constitutions of the UK and USA. [12]

Section B (comparative)

In your answer you must consider the relevance of at least one comparative theory.

5 Analyse the significant differences between the US and UK constitutions in their provision of checks and balances. [12]

6 Analyse the differences between the US and UK constitutions in their provision of democratic participation. [12]

Section C (USA)

In your answer you must consider the stated view and the alternative to this view in a balanced way.

7 Evaluate the extent to which the US Constitution provides adequately for ongoing amendment. [30]

8 Evaluate the extent to which the states are dominated by the federal government. [30]

Answers and quick quiz online

Revision activity

On a piece of card, draw out the two stages of the constitutional amendment process (make sure you include all four alternatives).

Exam skills

When you are asked to **'Evaluate'** in an exam question, you are expected to cover both sides of the argument and reach a considered judgement one way or the other.

- In question 7 above, for example, you need to discuss the ways in which the US Constitution **does** adequately provide for amendments.
- You also need to discuss the ways in which the US Constitution **does not** provide an adequate amendment process.
- You might then come to the conclusion that, given the small number of amendments that have been passed, the amendment process is not efficient. Or you might conclude that the small number of amendments that have been passed is evidence that the amendment process is effective as it prevents frivolous or unsafe meddling with the Constitution.

2 Congress

The structure of Congress

Congress is bicameral: it is made up of two houses — the House of Representatives and the Senate. This was part of the compromise made by the Founding Fathers at the Philadelphia Convention in 1787. Thus in the House of Representatives the number of members for each state is proportional of their population, while in the Senate each state has two members regardless of population.

Remember

'Congress' refers to the institution as a whole, i.e. both the Senate and the House together.

Other basic facts you need to know about Congress are as follows:

- The House has always been directly elected; the Senate only since 1914.
- Members of the House serve two-year terms; senators serve six-year terms with one-third being elected every two years. This means that there are congressional midterm elections two years into the president's term — these elections are important as they provide an indication of the popularity of the president and the president's party at the time. They are also important because they can change control of the House, the Senate or both chambers — making it easier or harder for the president to successfully pursue their political agenda, depending on whether their party has a majority in either or both chambers.
- The number of representatives for each state in the House is reapportioned after every ten-yearly census.
- Senators represent the entire state; members of the House represent a sub-division of the state called a congressional district — except in those states with only one House member.
- Incumbency is an important factor in Senate elections — the incumbent candidate has an automatic advantage over any possible rival candidate for the position. Better fundraising opportunities, experience in the office and better name recognition are all factors which mean that almost all Senate elections are won by the incumbent candidate.

Midterm elections Elections for the whole of the House and one-third of the Senate that occur midway through a president's four-year term.

Incumbency The holding of an office, position or role.

Incumbent A person who currently holds an office.

The composition of Congress is outlined in Table 2.1.

Table 2.1 Composition of Congress

House of Representatives	Senate
Lower house	Upper house
435 members	100 members
Represent a congressional district	Represent the entire state
Serve two-year terms	Serve six-year terms
Must be at least 25 years old	Must be at least 30 years old
Must have been a US citizen for at least seven years	Must have been a US citizen for at least nine years
Must be a resident of the state they represent	Must be a resident of the state they represent

Remember

It's not likely that you will need to list every difference between the two houses of Congress — but you should be able to describe general categories of difference (e.g. that there are different age and residency requirements for each chamber).

Female and minority ethnic representation

REVISED

Even as recently as the 1980s, Congress was composed almost exclusively of white men. Only in the past two or three decades has the representation of women and members of ethnic minorities increased significantly. In January 2021, in terms of women:

- There were 142 women in Congress, up from 127 before the 2020 elections.
- Of these, 118 were in the House and 24 in the Senate.

- That still means that only just over 26% of members of Congress were women.
- Of these 142 women, 106 were Democrats and just 36 Republicans.
- Following the 2020 elections, the number of women in the House who are Republicans increased from 13 to 28.

In terms of ethnic minorities:

- 58 members of Congress (11%) were black Americans — 55 in the House, 3 in the Senate.
- 50 members of Congress (9%) were Hispanic/Latino — 45 in the House, 5 in the Senate.
- 21 members of Congress (4%) were Asian — 19 in the House, 2 in the Senate.

In the country as a whole, the Census Bureau estimated that in 2019:

- 14.7% of the population were black Americans.
- 18.0% were Hispanic/Latino.
- 5.9% were Asian.

Therefore all these racial groups are under-represented in Congress, especially Hispanic and Latino Americans.

Party dominance

REVISED

In terms of party, both houses are dominated by the Republican and Democratic parties:

- Between 2001 and the end of 2022, the House has been controlled by the Democrats for 8 years and the Republicans for 14 years.
- During the same period, the Senate has been controlled by the Republicans for just over 10½ years and by the Democrats for just over 11½ years.
- Only two of Congress's 535 members belong to neither party — senators Bernie Sanders (Vermont) and Angus King (Maine) — but both almost always vote with the Democrats.

Now test yourself

TESTED 

1. How many houses make up Congress?
2. How many members are there in each?
3. How is the membership of each house distributed among the 50 states?
4. How many women and members of racial minorities were in each house in January 2021?
5. To what extent do the two major parties dominate Congress?

Answers on p. 112

The functions and powers of Congress

Congress has many formal, constitutional powers, three of which are the most important because they are most frequently used.

1. **Law making**:
   - Both houses have equal power.
   - All bills must pass through all stages in both houses.
   - Neither house can override the wishes of the other.
   - Both houses must agree to the proposed law in exactly the same form before it can be sent to the president.
   - All money bills (tax bills) must begin in the House.
2. **Overseeing the executive branch (investigation)**:
   - This is an implied power of the Constitution.
   - Congress has oversight of executive departments and agencies — it controls their budgets.
   - Oversight is conducted in standing and select committees.

Remember

This quotation shows how Congress derives its law-making function from the US Constitution:

'The Congress shall have power … to make all laws which shall be necessary and proper for carrying into execution … powers vested by this Constitution.' (The US Constitution)

3 **Confirming appointments**:
- Appointments are confirmed by the Senate only.
- Senate confirms the president's appointments to the federal judiciary and executive.
- The most important appointments are those to the Supreme Court and to the president's cabinet.
- A simple majority is required.
- Appointments are rarely rejected.

A second tier of powers includes the following.

4 **Overriding the president's veto**:
- This requires a two-thirds majority in both houses.
- It is very difficult to achieve.
- President Obama vetoed 12 bills in his eight years — just one was overridden.
- President Trump vetoed 10 bills in his four years — only one (his last) was overridden.

5 **Ratifying treaties**:
- Ratification is done by the Senate only.
- It requires a two-thirds majority.
- Treaties are rarely rejected.

The other powers of Congress are:

6 Initiating constitutional amendments.
7 Impeaching, trying and removing public officials.
8 Confirming an appointed vice president (used only in 1973 and 1974).
9 Declaring war (not used since 1941).
10 Electing the president (House) and vice president (Senate) if the Electoral College is deadlocked (not used since 1824).

Remember

If discussing the powers of Congress, don't forget to say that confirming appointments is a power only of the Senate.

Remember

Say that a two-thirds majority is required, but don't forget to say 'in both houses'.

Remember

The term 'impeachment' is often misunderstood. It simply means to make a formal accusation against someone. It does not mean to remove someone from office, though it may lead to that.

Remember

If asked a question about the powers of Congress, it is better to focus on the most important ones rather than trying to cover all ten. Perhaps cover the first three in detail, the next two with an example each, and then just mention one or two of the others.

Now test yourself TESTED

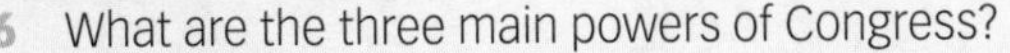

6 What are the three main powers of Congress?
7 What does the term 'impeachment' mean?
8 What majorities are required (a) to confirm appointments, (b) to override the president's veto and (c) to ratify treaties?

Answers on p. 113

The distribution of powers within Congress

It is usually suggested that the Senate is **more powerful** than the House because of:
- its exclusive power to confirm appointments
- its exclusive power to ratify treaties

It is usually suggested that the Senate is **more prestigious** than the House because:
- senators represent the entire state
- senators serve longer terms — six years as opposed to two years for House representatives

- senators are one of only 100
- senators are more likely to chair a committee or sub-committee
- the Senate is seen as a recruiting pool for the presidency and the vice presidency (see Tables 2.2 and 2.3)

Therefore House members often seek election to the Senate but not the other way around — in 2017 there were 50 former House members in the Senate but no former senators in the House.

However, it must be remembered that both chambers are equal in:

- passing legislation
- conducting oversight of the executive
- initiating constitutional amendments
- fulfilling a representative function
- their level of salaries

Remember

Don't forget the ways in which both chambers are equal.

Table 2.2 Serving and former senators who ran as Democratic presidential candidates in 2020

+ Michael Bennet (Colorado) + Cory Booker (New Jersey) + Kirsten Gillibrand (New York) + Kamala Harris (California)	+ Amy Klobuchar (Minnesota) + Bernie Sanders (Vermont) + Elizabeth Warren (Massachusetts)

Remember

Harris, Sanders and Warren are the better known of these candidates, but try to use at least one of the lesser known if you are asked for an example.

Table 2.3 Former senators who served as vice president, 1977–2021

Vice president	Party	Dates in office
Walter Mondale	Democratic	1977–81
Dan Quayle	Republican	1989–93
Al Gore	Democratic	1993–2001
Joe Biden	Democratic	2009–17
Kamala Harris	Democratic	2021–

Now test yourself TESTED

9 What are the two important exclusive powers of the Senate?

10 Give three reasons why the Senate is regarded as more prestigious than the House.

11 Give three ways in which the Senate and House are equal.

12 Give two examples of serving or former senators who ran for the presidency in 2020.

13 Name two recent vice presidents who had previously served in the Senate.

Answers on p. 113

The committee system and oversight

The four most important types of committee in Congress are:

1. Standing committees
2. House Rules Committee
3. Conference committees
4. Select committees

Remember

Watch that you don't misspell the word 'committee' — two 'm's, two 't's and two 'e's.

Standing committees

REVISED

Standing committees:

- exist in both houses (e.g. House Judiciary Committee, Senate Foreign Relations Committee)
- are mostly divided into sub-committees
- have around 18 members in the Senate, around 30–40 members in the House
- have three main functions:
  - conducting the committee stage of bills
  - conducting investigations
  - beginning the process of confirming appointments (Senate committees only)

The party balance of each committee reflects the party balance of the respective chamber.

Standing committee A permanent, policy-specialist committee of Congress playing key roles in both legislation and investigation.

Compare

The UK system also has standing committees, but this title refers to *ad hoc* committees in Parliament rather than permanent bodies. Can you give an example of a UK standing committee?

Conducting the committee stage of bills

Standing committees:

- scrutinise bills in their particular policy area
- hold hearings on the bill
- call witnesses to give evidence at their hearings
- have full power of amendment

Conducting investigations

Standing committees:

- investigate issues within their particular policy area
- investigate perceived problems, crises, policy failures
- oversee relevant executive departments and agencies
- call witnesses to appear at hearings
- can be high profile and influential

Beginning confirmation process (Senate only)

Standing committees:

- hold hearings on executive branch appointments made by the president within their particular policy area
- vote on whether or not to recommend the full Senate confirm a nominee (see Table 2.4).

The Senate Judiciary Committee also considers all presidential nominations to the federal judiciary.

Table 2.4 Standing committee votes on selected Biden cabinet officers, 2021

Post	Nominee	Standing committee
Secretary of Defense	Lloyd Austin	Armed Services
Secretary of State	Antony Blinken	Foreign Relations
Secretary of the Treasury	Janet Yellen	Finance
Attorney General	Merrick Garland	Judiciary

Revision activity

Using the internet, find out the results of the votes for each of the candidates in Table 2.4.

Making links

The need for congressional committees to ratify presidential executive and judiciary appointments is a power vested in Congress by the Constitution (see Chapter 1) and sometimes attracts a great deal of media attention and lobbying by interest groups (see Chapter 7) in a bid to influence the outcome.

House Rules Committee

REVISED

This committee:

- is one of the standing committees in the House but performs a totally different function from the others
- is responsible for prioritising bills coming from the committee stage on to the floor of the House for debate and votes
- gives a 'rule' to a bill that sets out the rules of debate, stating whether or not further amendments are permitted
- has just 13 members — 9 from the majority party, 4 from the minority party
- is highly influential: 'the legislative gate-keeper' of the House

Conference committees

REVISED 

These committees:

- are *ad hoc* (temporary)
- are made up of members from both chambers
- are set up to reconcile differences between House and Senate versions of a bill
- need to make compromises agreeable to a majority of both houses
- are important because they will often draw up the final version of the bill — but their compromise version must be passed by a majority vote in both houses

Remember

Although a conference committee has members from both chambers, don't confuse them with joint committees, which are mainly used for administrative purposes only.

Select committees

REVISED 

These committees:

- are also known as 'special' or 'investigative' committees
- are mostly *ad hoc*
- are used when an investigation does not fall within the policy area of one standing committee, or when the investigation is likely to be particularly time consuming (see Table 2.5).

Compare

The UK system also has select committees, but in the UK the title refers to permanent committees rather than *ad hoc* ones. Can you give an example of such a committee in the UK?

Table 2.5 Summary of the importance of congressional committees

Type of committee	They are important because they:
Standing committees	+ are regarded as policy specialists + conduct the committee stage of bills, which comes before the main debate in either chamber + conduct high-profile investigations + (in the Senate) begin the confirmation process of numerous presidential nominations
House Rules Committee	+ control the passage of bills from the committees to the floor in the House + decide the terms of debate for each bill (e.g. whether or not amendments are permitted) + are seen as the 'gate-keeper' of the legislative process in the House
Conference committees	+ come right at the end of the legislative process + have almost life or death power over a bill + often write what will be the final version of the bill
Select committees	+ conduct high-profile and often long-running investigations

Remember

Try to learn the name of at least one example of each type of committee to use in an exam answer on the legislative process.

Congressional caucuses are also common in the US Congress. They meet regularly to discuss their concerns and coordinate their activities. There are several types of congressional caucuses, including ideological, party, racial and even geographical — southern Democrats, for example, might create a caucus to discuss specific issues or concerns of southern voters.

Congressional caucuses Also called 'conferences', congressional caucuses are groups of politicians who share the same interests and views, usually from the same political party.

Now test yourself

TESTED

14 Name three different types of congressional committee.
15 How many members typically make up a standing committee in each house?
16 How is the party balance of each standing committee decided?
17 What functions do standing committees have?
18 Give an example of a standing committee vote on President Biden's cabinet nominees.
19 What does the House Rules Committee do?
20 What is the function of a conference committee?
21 Why would a select committee be set up?

Answers on p. 113

Congress and representation

Models of representation

REVISED

Different models are used to describe how legislators represent their constituents. These are outlined in Table 2.6.

For further information on congressional elections, see Chapter 6.

Table 2.6 Representation in Congress

Model	How legislators represent their constituents
Trustee model	✚ Legislator makes decisions on behalf of constituents — the legislator is acting as a 'trustee'. ✚ Legislator uses their 'mature judgement'.
Delegate model	✚ Legislator makes decisions to reflect the views of the majority of their constituents. ✚ Legislator does not exercise their own judgement.

Representation Either how legislators represent their constituents or who the legislators are and whether they are 'representative' of constituents in terms of, for example, gender and race.

Remember

If answering a question on 'representation' in Congress, always make sure that you clearly define the term, explaining the differences in Table 2.6.

Most members of Congress will probably see their representative role as a blend of both models, though House members — subject to a two-yearly election cycle — will tend to lean more to putting a higher premium on constituents' views.

How well legislators represent their constituents can also be considered in terms of whether legislators are representative in their:

- gender
- race
- age
- socio-economic class
- previous occupation
- education

While there have been some significant attempts at increasing the representativeness of Congress — with greater numbers of women and ethnic minorities standing for election and taking office — the fact remains that there is very little diversity within the legislature.

Engagement with constituents

REVISED

Members of Congress engage with their constituents through many different methods and channels, including:

- holding party and town hall meetings
- conducting 'surgeries' with individual constituents
- making visits around the state/district

- appearing on local radio phone-ins
- taking part in interviews with local media
- addressing various groups in their state/district (e.g. chambers of commerce, Rotary Clubs)
- using email and social media

Debate

How adequate is Congress at fulfilling its representative function?

Arguments that it is adequate	Arguments that it is not adequate
+ Elections are frequent (especially in the House). + There is a constitutional requirement that members of Congress must reside in the state they represent (and a locality rule for House members in many states). + Constituents can now share their views with members of Congress in a large number of ways.	+ Constituents' views on many issues are very divided. + Many members of Congress see themselves more as 'trustees' than 'delegates'. + In today's era of hyper-partisanship, following the party line often trumps constituency representation as the main cue in voting.

Remember

You might be asked about how effective Congress is in general or more specifically about how effective it is at representation, for example. You therefore need to be confident in your knowledge of all of the functions of Congress, and its effectiveness at each function.

Now test yourself

TESTED 

22 Explain the two different interpretations of the word 'representation'.

23 Explain the difference between the trustee and delegate models of representation.

24 Give four ways in which members of Congress engage with constituents.

Answers on p. 113

Congress and legislation

The legislative process in Congress is best thought of in six stages, as shown in Table 2.7.

Table 2.7 The six stages of the legislative process in Congress

Stage	What happens
1 Introduction	+ A formality + Between 10,000 and 14,000 bills introduced in a typical Congress (two years) + Only about 2–4% of those will become law
2 Committee stage	+ The most important stage + Comes before the full chamber has debated the bill + Conducted by the relevant standing committee (see page 25) + Committees hold hearings on bills + Have full power of amendment + After hearings, committee writes report, which recommends future action + However, most bills never get any further
3 Timetabling	+ In the House, by the House Rules Committee (see page 26) + In the Senate, by **unanimous consent** agreement
4 Floor debate and vote	+ Further amendments are possible + Votes are taken: either voice votes or recorded votes + In the Senate, a **filibuster** is possible, which can be ended by a successful **cloture motion**
5 Conference committee	+ Used to reconcile the differences between the House and Senate versions of the bill (see page 26) + But this work is now often done behind the scenes by an *ad hoc*, leadership-driven group

6 Presidential action	+ The president has four options:
	  + Sign the bill into law
	  + Leave the bill on their desk (it becomes law within ten working days)
	  + **Presidential veto** (Congress may override with two-thirds majorities in both houses)
	  + **Pocket veto** (usable only at the end of the legislative session)

Unanimous consent A legislative process whereby a legislator requests approval by all representatives to a rule change or law, without requiring a formal vote.

Filibuster A device by which one or more senators can delay action on a bill or any other matter by debating it at length or through other obstructive actions.

Cloture motion A vote to bring about the end of a filibuster, requiring a supermajority of senators in order to succeed.

Presidential veto The president's power under Article II of the Constitution to return a bill to Congress unsigned, along with the reasons for the objection.

Pocket veto A veto power exercised by the president at the end of a legislative session whereby bills not signed are lost.

Compare

The legislative process in Westminster is very similar to that of the USA. Can you think of any differences?

Remember

If answering a question about Congress's law-making function, don't just plough through the six stages of the legislative process — select carefully what information is actually needed to answer the question you've been asked.

On average, only between 3% and 4% of bills that are introduced into Congress are actually passed into law. So that raises the question: 'How effective is Congress in fulfilling its legislative function?' There are arguments on both sides.

Debate

How effective is Congress in fulfilling its legislative function?

Arguments that it is effective	Arguments that it is not effective
+ The process is deliberately designed to be complicated and to weed out unpopular legislation. + An average of 300 new Acts of Congress signed into law every two years is still quite a lot — especially considering all the new laws that are passed by the 50 state legislatures. + 'Limited government' is a founding principle of the US political system — a belief that government should act only when it is essential. + Congress has passed some significant pieces of legislation in recent decades relating to gun violence, free trade, education, campaign finance, economic recovery and healthcare reform.	+ The procedures of Congress often mean that the will of the majority can be frustrated by a well-organised minority (e.g. power of committee chairs, filibustering, need for supermajorities) + The small-population states are over-represented in the Senate. + The two-yearly election cycle in the House means members spend too much time fundraising and campaigning, and not enough time on legislation. + Congress spends a lot of time debating and voting on bills of minor importance (e.g. allowing the Postal Service to issue a commemorative stamp).

Remember

In the exam you may be asked to reach a conclusion on how effective Congress is. Be prepared with a judgement and with examples to back up your argument. Make sure you can demonstrate awareness of both sides of the argument.

Now test yourself TESTED

25 Why is the committee stage of a bill so important?

26 What is a filibuster?

27 What options does the president have when receiving a bill?

28 Explain the terms (a) presidential veto and (b) pocket veto.

29 How can Congress override a presidential veto?

Answers on p. 113

Congress and oversight

Congress carries out its oversight function through:

+ standing committee hearings
+ the subpoena of documents and testimony
+ the Senate's power to confirm appointments
+ the Senate's power to ratify treaties

There are no executive branch members present in the legislature, so oversight work is conducted mostly in the standing committees of both houses.

Oversight Congressional review and investigation of the activities of the executive branch of government.

Subpoena A summons or demand for something.

Debate

How effective is Congress in fulfilling its oversight function?

Arguments that it is effective	Arguments that it is not effective
+ Appearances by senior members of the executive branch at congressional committee hearings are a real check on their power. + Oversight hearings often receive high levels of media coverage. + Presidential nominations to the executive and judicial branches can be dealt death blows by Senate standing committees. + Committee members are policy experts in their own fields and therefore can ask searching questions.	+ Members of the president's party may ask 'soft ball' questions during hearings. + Members of the opposition party may indulge in partisan point-scoring rather than effective oversight. + Committees rarely vote to reject presidential nominees to the executive and judicial branches. + Lengthy hearings do not necessarily result in effective oversight (e.g. House Republican hearings on the terrorist attack in Benghazi, 2012).

Compare

As in the USA, the UK legislature has oversight powers and responsibilities over the executive. Can you think of three ways in which Parliament has oversight of the executive in the UK?

Now test yourself

TESTED 

30 What is meant by the term 'oversight'?

31 Give two ways in which Congress carries out this function.

32 Why is oversight carried out in committees rather than in the chambers?

Answers on p. 113

Voting in Congress

There are five main factors that affect voting in Congress:

1 Parties and caucuses
2 The administration
3 Interest groups
4 Lobbyists
5 Constituents

We consider these below.

Parties and caucuses

REVISED

There has been much increased party unity within congressional parties during the past two decades. However, parties have few, if any, incentives or disincentives to encourage party-line voting. Those members who stray from the party line may find themselves faced by a primary challenger in the next election cycle.

Compare

Whips exist in both the UK and the US systems. They are, however, much more powerful in the UK Parliament than in the US Congress. In what ways do whips influence MPs and congressmen and women?

The administration

REVISED

The president, vice president, senior members of the White House staff and the president's congressional liaison staff all lobby members of Congress to support them on key votes. Cabinet members lobby in their respective policy areas.

Success for the administration depends on a number of variables:

- the size of the president's mandate at the last election
- the president's current approval rating in the country
- the first term — this tends to be more successful than the second term
- the president's persuasive skills and relationship with their own party in Congress

> **Making links**
>
> Since the 1930s an approval rating has been given to presidents based on periodic polling of sample voters. A typical question is: 'Do you approve or disapprove of the way the current president is handling their job as president?' The approval rating is measured by the percentage of those questioned who approve of the work the president is doing. This approval rating can be influential on the way the public view the president and can impact on their voting in presidential, congressional and midterm elections (see Chapter 6).

Interest groups

Interest groups try to influence how members of Congress vote:

- through direct contact with key members (e.g. at committee hearings)
- by generating public support for the positions they favour
- by organising rallies, demonstrations, etc.
- through fundraising and campaigning

Lobbyists

Interest groups or other organisations, including large businesses, may employ the services of professional lobbyists. Lobbyists have strong political ties and were often politicians themselves. They generally represent the interests of their client in order to persuade members of Congress to vote in a specific way. Former members of Congress are often sought after by lobbying companies as they have valuable political contacts and networks as well as name recognition in Washington, DC. For this reason, many retired members find a second career in lobbying once they have left the chamber.

Constituents

Members of Congress really never stop campaigning for the next election — especially members of the House, who only have a two-year term in office. This means that the views of constituents, and the impact a vote in Congress might have on their support, is a very important factor influencing voting behaviour.

> **Remember**
>
> Factors will vary from one member to another and from one vote to another. Most votes will be the result of a number of factors, not just one.

> **Now test yourself**
>
> 
>
> 33 Give three important factors that may determine the way members of Congress vote.
>
> 34 Give three examples of people/groups who may try to influence members of Congress on behalf of the administration.
>
> **Answers on p. 113**

Parties in Congress

The two major parties dominate Congress:
- Almost all members are either Democrats or Republicans.
- The major parties control all leadership positions.

The two major parties have each become more ideologically cohesive during the past two decades, whereas previously there were more similarities between parties. The parties in Congress are currently characterised by:
- an era of 'hyper-partisanship'
- greater unity within the parties, especially in the House (see Figure 2.1)
- more distinct conflicts between the parties
- strictly party-line votes on most big-ticket items (e.g. President Trump's tax cuts in December 2017 received no Democrat votes in either house)
- few 'centrists' being left in Congress

This makes bipartisanship and cooperation 'across the aisle' much more difficult than it was.

It often leads to gridlock.

This all represents a significant change from just a few decades ago when parties in Congress were not very important because:
- the Democrats and Republicans were at times almost indistinguishable from one another
- both contained 'liberals' and 'conservatives'
- a typical vote in Congress used to be one group of Democrats and Republicans voting against another group of Democrats and Republicans
- 'party unity' was very low, especially in the House (see Figure 2.1)
- both contained so-called 'centrists', who frequently participated in bipartisan votes
- the emphasis was then more on individual members and sub-groups of the parties rather than on the parties themselves
- the role of the party leadership was not very important or influential

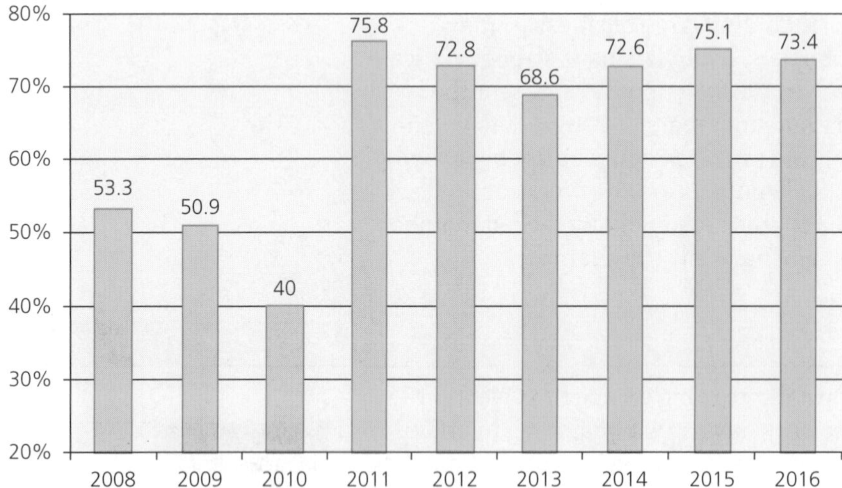

Figure 2.1 Party unity votes: House of Representatives, 2008–16

Note: Data indicate the percentage of all roll-call votes on which a majority of Democrats voted against a majority of Republicans.

Source: www.brookings.edu

Compare

The UK political system has moved on from being described as a 'two-party system' given the success of third and fourth parties in recent decades. However, to what extent would it be correct to describe the UK Parliament as being **dominated** by two parties?

Partisanship A situation where members of one party regularly group together to oppose members of another party, characterised by strong party discipline and little cooperation between the parties.

Gridlock Failure to get action on policy proposals and legislation in Congress. Gridlock is thought to be exacerbated by divided government and partisanship.

Debate

Do parties play an important role in Congress?

Yes	No
+ Leadership of Congress is controlled by the parties. + Committees in Congress are organised by the parties. + With increased partisanship, party discipline is much stronger in Congress than it used to be. + Party is an important determinant of voting in Congress. + It is almost impossible to be elected to Congress without being a major-party candidate.	+ Views of constituents can often outweigh party considerations — especially for House members. + Parties have no control over candidate selection. + Both parties are made up of ideological factions that challenge party cohesion. + The executive branch has few 'sticks or carrots' by which to incentivise party discipline. + Congressional leadership, likewise, is fairly impotent in the face of opposition.

Remember

You might be asked about whether parties play an important role in Congress, but you could also be asked to consider just one point of view (e.g. that parties do not play an important role). Make sure you understand what the question is asking you to do before you rush into an answer prepared in advance.

Now test yourself

TESTED

35 In what two ways do the two major parties dominate Congress?
36 Name two consequences of the two major parties having become more ideologically cohesive.
37 Explain the terms (a) partisanship and (b) gridlock.
38 What has happened to the number of 'centrists' in Congress?
39 Explain what the data in Figure 2.1 show.

Answers on pp. 113–14

Factors that influence the relationship between Congress and the presidency

There are seven factors that influence the relationship between Congress and the presidency:

1 Party control
2 Party polarisation
3 Policy area
4 Election cycle
5 Presidential poll rating
6 Congressional approval rating
7 National events

Party control

REVISED

Congressional oversight of the executive is only really effective when Congress is not controlled by the president's party.

Almost all modern-day examples of the Senate's rejection of presidential nominations, whether to the executive or judicial branches, have come when the president's party has not controlled the Senate. For example, it was a Republican Senate which, in 1999, rejected Democrat president Bill Clinton's nomination of Ronnie White to be a federal trial court judge and his Nuclear Test Ban Treaty.

In times of united government, oversight can drop considerably, which was demonstrated during President George W. Bush's eight-year term. Throughout most of the first six years (2001–06), Bush's Republican Party controlled both houses of Congress. During these years, congressional oversight was light, if not at times almost non-existent.

Party polarisation

REVISED

Party polarisation has seen the parties grow ideologically further and further apart since the 1980s. This often causes a strain in the relationship between parties and the president. This problem is exacerbated in divided government, but it would be a mistake to conclude that Congress and the president cannot come to agreement. The following Acts demonstrate bipartisanship:

- Jobs Act (2012)
- Bipartisan Budget Act (2013)
- Every Student Succeed Act (2015)
- Coronavirus Aid, Relief, and Economic Security (CARES) Act (2020)

Divided government
Where control of the executive branch (presidency) and the legislature (Congress) is split between two parties.

Policy area

REVISED

Congress's ability to influence the president is greater for domestic policy than it is for foreign policy.

In foreign policy, presidents frequently use executive agreements to circumnavigate the Senate.

- Obama was able to pass the Joint Comprehensive Plan of Action in 2015 concerning the Iranian nuclear programme with little oversight from the Senate.
- Similarly, Trump was able to abandon the Iran Nuclear Deal in 2018, again with little oversight from the Senate..

Election cycle

REVISED

When Congress is gearing up to elections, members are much more likely to be interested in pleasing their state or district than they are the president. This can be especially true if a president is unpopular or is about to leave office, when members of the president's party will prioritise their own re-election above the wishes of their president.

An excellent example of this was when Congress overrode Obama's veto of the Justice against Sponsors of Terrorism Bill in 2016. While many Democrats in both houses shared Obama's doubts over the efficacy of the legislation, they were loath to appear soft on terrorism weeks before the 2016 congressional elections. As an outgoing president, there was little Obama could do to persuade anyone to support his stance.

Presidential poll rating

REVISED

Congress is able to exert less influence on the president when presidential poll ratings are high but considerably more when the ratings are low.

- When President George W. Bush attempted to reform social security in 2005, Congress was able to capitalise on his low poll ratings to frustrate his attempts to pass social security reform. In February 2005, a Gallup Poll demonstrated that only 35% of Americans approved of Bush's handling of the reform, while 65% disapproved.
- Things were completely different in September 2001, when Bush enjoyed the highest presidential approval rating ever recorded, in the immediate aftermath of the 9/11 attacks. With a 90% approval rating, Congress's relationship with the president was almost subservient in this period and Bush was able to pass the Patriot Act (2001) as his administration began its 'war on terror' both at home and abroad.

Donald Trump's presidential approval ratings were the lowest of any president since the Second World War (averaging 41% over his term in office and never exceeding 49% in his entire presidency). This consistent lack of popularity made it easier for Congress to defy President Trump and the image of House Speaker Nancy Pelosi ripping up Trump's State of the Union address in February 2020 symbolised the fractious relationship between Congress and the president from 2016 to 2020.

Congressional approval rating

REVISED

Over recent years, Congress's standing in the eyes of the public has reached historic lows.

Congress is seen by Americans as self-interested and unproductive, given that it only averages a success rate of around 2–3% in passing new legislation.

National events

REVISED

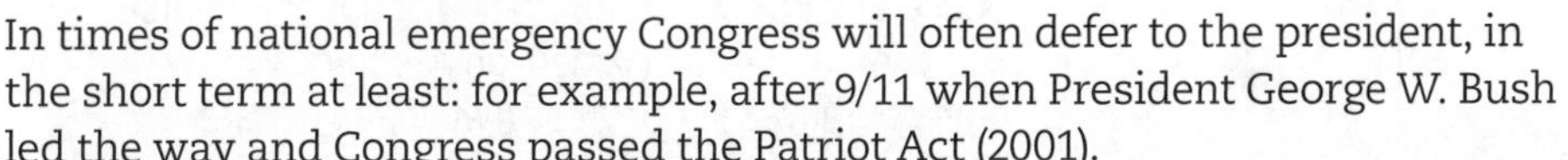

In times of national emergency Congress will often defer to the president, in the short term at least: for example, after 9/11 when President George W. Bush led the way and Congress passed the Patriot Act (2001).

However, this is not always the case. Although Congress assisted President Trump in passing the Coronavirus Aid, Relief and Economic Security (CARES) Act in March 2020, it had also been extremely critical of the President's handling of the crisis, with the Democrat House Speaker, Nancy Pelosi, regularly rebutting the President and acting as the leader of congressional opposition to his policies.

Comparing Congress with the UK Parliament

The differences between the US Congress and the UK Parliament are mainly the result of the fundamental structural differences between the two systems of government (see Table 2.8). Table 2.9 compares the similarities and differences.

Table 2.8 Summary of the structural differences between the US Congress and the UK Parliament

In the USA	In the UK
Members of Congress are not permitted to hold a post in the executive at the same time.	The executive branch personnel are drawn almost exclusively from Parliament.
The president and vice president are elected independently from members of Congress.	The prime minister is the elected leader of the largest party in the House of Commons.
Executive branch members can be removed by Congress only through impeachment.	The government's term can be ended by losing a vote of confidence in the House of Commons.
The president has few 'sticks and carrots' to encourage party discipline.	The prime minister can encourage party discipline through the power of patronage and the use of whips.

Remember

Table 2.8 is an example of the structural approach to comparative politics — make sure you reference this approach if possible.

Table 2.9 Comparing Congress and Parliament: similarities and differences

Similarities	Differences
+ Both are bicameral. + Different parties may control each house. + President/prime minister's party may not control both houses. + Both houses in both institutions have a role in passing legislation and in oversight of the executive. + Much work is done away from the chambers in committees. + Oversight function is conducted by the standing committees in Congress and by the select committees of the House of Commons. + All elections are on a first-past-the-post system.	+ Elections: Congress — both houses elected. Parliament — only one house elected. + Powers of chambers: Congress — two equal houses. Parliament — lower house dominates. + Parties: Congress — only two parties represented. Parliament — multiple parties, especially in House of Commons. + Executive: Congress — executive branch excluded. Parliament — executive branch included. + Terms of office: House of Representatives, 2 years; Senate, 6 years. House of Commons, 5 years. + Size of upper house: Senate — 100. House of Lords — around 800 (lower house is also significantly larger in the UK). + Oversight: Senate has oversight powers unknown to the House of Lords (e.g. confirmation of appointments). + Representation: Each American has three representatives in Congress (two in the Senate, one in the House). Each British person has only one representative in Parliament.

Composition of Congress and Parliament

REVISED

The differences between Congress and Parliament in terms of composition are mainly the result of the different structural and cultural backgrounds of the two nations (see Table 2.10).

Table 2.10 Structural and cultural differences affecting the composition of Congress and Parliament

In Congress	In Parliament
The institution reflects the federal structure of the USA.	The institution reflects the unitary/devolved structure of the UK.
Members of both houses represent states (Senate) or part of a state (House).	MPs represent the historic counties, cities and towns of the UK.
The directly elected upper chamber reflects the principle of democratic participation.	The hereditary/appointed upper chamber reflects a nation in which the landed gentry and the established church were dominant.

Revision activity

Highlight the points in Table 2.10 that are examples of a structural approach to comparative politics, and using a different colour do the same with those that are examples of a cultural approach.

Powers and functions of Congress and Parliament

REVISED

Legislation

In terms of dealing with legislation, there are significant differences between Congress and Parliament, mostly resulting from the structural differences between the two systems — one a presidential system based on the separation of powers; the other a parliamentary system based on a fusion of powers (see Table 2.11).

Table 2.11 Legislative function of Congress and Parliament compared

In Congress	In Parliament
No government programme of legislation exists.	A government programme of legislation dominates the agenda.
Level of party discipline is lower.	There are higher levels of party discipline.
Thousands of bills are introduced in any one session.	Limited number of bills are introduced in any one session.
Individual members introduce numerous pieces of legislation.	Individual members introduce few pieces of legislation.
Few of these bills are passed into law.	Most bills are passed into law.
Committee stage comes before the debate in the chamber.	Committee stage comes after the Second Reading debate in the chamber.
Standing committees are permanent and policy specialist.	Standing committees are non-permanent and non-specialist.
Bills are usually considered by both houses concurrently.	Bills are considered by the two houses consecutively.
Two chambers have equal powers.	Lower chamber dominates.
President has significant veto power.	The Royal Assent is no longer withheld.

Oversight

In terms of oversight of the executive branch, Congress and Parliament again have significant differences resulting from the structural differences between the two systems (see Table 2.12).

Table 2.12 Methods of oversight in Congress and Parliament compared

In Congress	In Parliament
+ Standing committee hearings + Select committee hearings + Confirmation of appointments (Senate) + Ratification of treaties (Senate) + Impeachment, trial, removal from office	+ Question time (including Prime Minister's Questions + Select committee hearings + Liaison Committee hearings + Correspondence with ministers + Tabling of early day motions + Policy debates + Office of the Ombudsman + Votes of no confidence

Representation

In terms of fulfilling their representative function, the differences between members of Congress and members of the House of Commons can best be understood by applying the rational choice approach, which highlights the way these two sets of legislators operate according to their self-interest. Members of the Senate, the House of Representatives and the House of Commons tend to fulfil their representative functions by considering who controls their electoral destiny — both at the nomination stage and in the election itself (see Table 2.13).

Table 2.13 Factors likely to influence members of Congress and members of the House of Commons in fulfilling their representative function

In Congress	In House of Commons
Members must face voters every two (House) or six (Senate) years.	Members must face voters at least every five years.
Nomination is in the hands of ordinary voters in the primary.	Nomination is in the hands of the local party members.

Revision activity

Evaluate the importance of each of the factors in Table 2.13 in influencing members of Congress and the House of Commons.

Comparing the two lower chambers

REVISED

Both the House of Representatives and the House of Commons are directly elected, but that is about as far as the similarities go. The differences are numerous (see Table 2.14).

Table 2.14 The two lower chambers compared

House of Representatives	House of Commons
Members serve a maximum term of two years.	Members serve a maximum term of five years.
Term is fixed by the Constitution (entrenched).	Term is fixed by Act of Parliament, but with provisos.
Only two parties are represented.	Eight parties are currently represented.
No executive branch members.	Includes executive branch members.
Shares equal legislative power with upper chamber.	Has ultimate legislative power on most matters.
Members represent numerically equal electoral districts.	Members represent numerically unequal electoral districts.
Focus of the legislative process is the standing committees.	Focus of the legislative process is the floor of the chamber.
Committee stage comes before floor debate.	Committee stage comes after floor debate.
Legislative committees are permanent and policy specialist.	Legislative committees are *ad hoc*.
Oversight of the executive takes place only in committee rooms.	Oversight of the executive takes place both in the chamber and in committee rooms.
The Speaker is a partisan figure.	The Speaker is a neutral umpire of debate.
Members seek elevation to the upper chamber to advance their political careers.	Senior members 'retire' to the upper chamber.

Revision activity

Take three of the rows in the above table. Use the contents of both columns of these rows to write a fuller paragraph to discuss three comparisons between the two lower chambers. Consider the three comparative approaches — rational, cultural and structural — in your answer.

Comparing the two upper chambers

REVISED

When it comes to the two upper chambers, the differences are so great that comparison becomes quite difficult (see Table 2.15).

Table 2.15 The two upper chambers compared

Senate	House of Lords
Directly elected (since 1914)	By appointment or heredity
100 members	Around 800 sitting members
Members serve six-year terms	Most serve for life
Dominated by only two parties	Includes a significant number of members who are non-partisan, crossbenchers, bishops)
Has equal legislative power with lower chamber	Essentially has only a delaying power over legislation
Has power to confirm executive and judicial appointments	Has no power to confirm executive and judicial appointments
Has power to ratify treaties	Has no power to ratify treaties
Seen as a recruiting ground for presidents and vice presidents	Seen as a retirement post for long-serving politicians
Has equal oversight powers with lower house	Oversight powers seen as less important than those of the lower house

Now test yourself

TESTED

40 Give two structural differences between Congress and Parliament.

41 Give four similarities and four differences between Congress and Parliament.

42 Give two differences, either structural or cultural, that affect the composition of Congress and Parliament.

43 Give four differences in the ways that Congress and Parliament deal with legislation.

44 Name four methods that Congress and Parliament use to perform their oversight function.

45 Give four ways in which the House of Representatives and the House of Commons differ.

46 Give four ways in which the Senate and the House of Lords differ.

Answers on p. 114

Summary

You should now have an understanding of:

- the structure and composition of Congress
- the powers of Congress
- the importance of congressional committees
- the effectiveness of Congress in legislation, oversight and representation
- voting in Congress
- the role of parties in Congress
- the similarities and differences between Congress and the UK Parliament

Exam practice

Section A (comparative)

1 Examine the ways in which the US Senate and the UK House of Lords differ. [12]

2 Examine the ways in which the US Congress and the UK Parliament pass legislation. [12]

Section B (comparative)

In your answer you must consider the relevance of at least one comparative theory.

3 Analyse the ways in which the US Congress and the UK Parliament perform their oversight function. [12]

4 Analyse the ways in which members of the US House of Representatives and the UK House of Commons perform their representative function. [12]

Section C (USA)

In your answer you must consider the stated view and the alternative to this view in a balanced way.

5 Evaluate the extent to which the Senate is more powerful and prestigious than the House. [30]

6 Evaluate the extent to which Congress is an effective legislative body. [30]

7 Evaluate the extent to which congressional oversight of the presidency is limited. [30]

Answers and quick quiz online

Revision activity

Compose a 30-mark examination question that is not one of those listed here. Remember it needs to have 'Evaluate' as a command word. The question must be based on the contents of this chapter. Either alone or with a partner, produce an essay plan to answer the question you have set.

Exam skills

If an exam question asks you to **'Examine**...' something you need to take apart, describe and explain the factors that you are being asked to examine. So, in question 1 above, you are being asked to examine the ways in which the US Senate and the UK House of Lords differ. This question is worth 12 marks. You need to determine all the ways that the two chambers differ, then 'examine' each of those differences — take each one, describe the difference and explain it, perhaps by explaining why it is a difference or by elaborating with an example.

3 The presidency

The formal powers of the president

The Constitution gives the president ten powers, outlined in Table 3.1.

Table 3.1 The ten powers of the president

1 Propose legislation	+ Often uses the annual State of the Union Address to Congress + For example, Trump (2018) announced a plan to spend $1.5 trillion on infrastructure + This power also includes submission of annual budget
2 Sign legislation	+ May hold bill-signing ceremony to claim credit + For example, Trump tax cuts (2017)
3 Veto legislation	+ Even the threat of a veto is a significant power + When used, the president usually prevails — Trump won 9 of his 10 vetoes (2017–21)
4 Act as chief executive	+ In charge of running the **executive branch** + Is head of government + Assisted by cabinet: department and agency heads + Executive Office of the President (EXOP)
5 Nominate executive branch officials	+ Department and agency heads + For example, Trump appointed Mike Pompeo as Secretary of State (2018)
6 Nominate federal judges	+ Including Supreme Court justices + For example, Trump appointed Brett Kavanaugh (2018) and Amy Coney Barrett (2020)
7 Act as commander-in-chief	+ Has overall control of the armed forces — this was especially important from the 1940s to the 1980s during the Cold War hostilities with the Soviet Union + For example, Bill Clinton ordered the bombing of Kosovo in 1999 and Barack Obama presided over extensive bombing in Libya which led to the downfall of the Gadhafi regime
8 Negotiate treaties	+ Symbolises the peace-making role alongside the commander-in-chief role
9 Pardon and commutation of prison sentence	+ Controversial power, especially when used to benefit close friends and supporters + Bill Clinton made a total of 140 pardons while in office, Barack Obama 212 and Donald Trump 237
10 Act as head of state	+ Is the public face or representative of the nation, both internationally and in **domestic politics**

Executive branch The branch of government that has responsibility for exercising authority across the governed territory and for implementing and enforcing the laws created by the legislative branch.

Domestic politics The decisions and policies that the executive and legislature make that are specifically to do with issues or events within a country.

Compare

There are certain powers that both the US president and the British prime minister have, but others that are unique to the president. Using two different colours, highlight which of the powers in Table 3.1 are applicable to both and which are unique to the USA.

Now test yourself TESTED

1 What powers does the president have concerning legislation?

Remember

If asked about the powers of the president in an exam question, you will need to group powers together so as not to have too many points to deal with: for example, 1. legislative powers (1–3); 2. executive powers (4); 3. appointment powers (5–6); 4. foreign policy powers (7–8); 5. head of state powers (9–10).

2 What is the president's annual address to Congress called?
3 What appointment powers does the president have? Give two examples.
4 What foreign policy powers does the president have?

Answers on p. 114

The vice president

REVISED

The vice president is elected on a joint ticket with the president — for example, Donald Trump and Mike Pence in 2016, and Joe Biden and Kamala Harris in 2020.

The president can fill a vacancy in the vice presidency by appointment, as has occurred twice (Gerald Ford in 1973; Nelson Rockefeller in 1974). This appointment must be confirmed by Congress.

The Constitution gives the vice president five powers (see Table 3.2).

Table 3.2 The five powers of the vice president

1 Presiding officer of the Senate	+ Chairs debates (but usually this is done by junior members of the majority party)
2 Voting in the case of a tied vote in the Senate	+ Vice President Mike Pence voted 13 times in the Senate, more than all except 6 of the 36 vice presidents who have held the office since 1789
3 Counting the Electoral College votes after the presidential election	+ Mike Pence presided over the counting of the Electoral College votes in January 2021 following the 2020 election
4 Becoming president in the event of the death, resignation or removal of the president	+ Has occurred on nine occasions + Vice President Gerald Ford became president when President Nixon resigned (1974)
5 Becoming acting president if the president is declared, or declares himself, disabled (by the Twenty-Fifth Amendment)	+ Vice President Dick Cheney twice became acting president while President George W. Bush underwent exploratory surgery

Making links

The US Constitution states that, to be eligible for the vice president position, a person must be a natural-born citizen, at least 35 years of age, and have been resident in the USA for at least 14 years.

It is clearly the second, fourth and fifth of these powers that give the vice president the most potential significance.

Now test yourself TESTED

5 How is the vice president elected?
6 What happens if the vice presidency falls vacant?
7 What are the two most significant powers of the vice president?

Answers on p. 114

Informal sources of presidential power

Informal powers of the president come from sources not mentioned in the Constitution as well as outside factors over which the president has limited control (see Table 3.3).

Table 3.3 The sources of the informal powers of the president

Informal source of presidential power	Details
The cabinet	An advisory group set up by the president to aid in making decisions and coordinating the work of the federal government.
Executive Office of the President (EXOP)	Contains the top staff agencies in the White House that assist the president in carrying out the major responsibilities of the presidential office.
White House Office (WHO)	Part of EXOP, the WHO is the personal office of the president containing the staff who facilitate the president's communication with Congress, department and agency heads, the press and public.
National Security Council (NSC)	Part of EXOP, the NSC is the president's official forum for deliberating national security and foreign policy.
Office of Management and Budget (OMB)	The office within EXOP that reviews budget requests, legislative initiatives, and proposed rules and regulations from the executive departments and agencies.
Powers of persuasion	The president uses personal influence, authority of office and political capital, and makes deals to obtain the support of key political actors.
Executive orders	Issued as a form of direct authority. They are often used by presidents frustrated by congressional resistance to their agenda as an alternative to legislation.
Executive agreements	Agreements between the president and a foreign nation, often used as alternatives to formal treaties.
Signing statements	Statements issued by the president on signing a bill which may challenge specific provisions of the bill on constitutional or other grounds.
Electoral mandate	The larger the president's electoral mandate, the more likely they are to achieve their legislative agenda.
Public approval	The president's public approval rating can affect their ability to get things done.
National events	National events can affect presidential power, enhancing or weakening their position in relation to Congress, the states and the president's personal approval ratings. For example, the aftermath of the 9/11 terrorist attacks increased the popularity of George W. Bush, whereas the handling of the Covid-19 pandemic negatively affected Donald Trump's approval rating.

Informal powers Political rather than constitutional powers.

Powers of persuasion Using personal influence to convince others to provide support.

Electoral mandate The size of the majority won by the president at the election — the higher the majority, the bigger the electoral mandate.

Cabinet The advisory group selected by the president to assist in making decisions and coordinating the work of the federal government.

The cabinet

REVISED

The cabinet is not mentioned in the Constitution.

- Article II states that the president 'may require the opinion in writing' of the heads of each executive department.
- It is an advisory and coordinating, not a decision-making, group.

Membership and appointment

The heads of the 15 executive departments are traditionally members of the cabinet, plus others whom the president designates as having cabinet rank (e.g. US Trade Representative).

- In 2017, Trump had eight such additional members, plus the vice president.
- It is difficult to recruit cabinet members from incumbent members of Congress as they must then resign from Congress.
- Cabinet members are drawn from former members of Congress, state governors, big-city mayors, academia, etc.
- They tend to be policy specialists.
- Appointments must be confirmed by a majority vote in the Senate.
- Ideally presidents would appoint a cabinet that is balanced in terms of:
  - gender
  - race
  - region
  - age
  - ideology
- However, the cabinet often looks like the president in terms of these criteria (e.g. the Trump cabinet was mainly white, male, older, wealthy business executives).

Compare

In theory both a president and a prime minister are free to choose whomever they want to join their cabinet. In reality, what constraints exist for them both?

Meetings

Frequency of cabinet meetings varies from one president to another.

- Trump held nine in 2017 (well above the recent average).
- Presidents tend to hold fewer cabinet meetings as their presidency progresses. Trump held only two full cabinet meetings in his final year in office – 19 May and 16 December 2020.
- Cabinet meetings can fulfil different functions for the president:
  - Engender team spirit
  - Promote collegiality
  - Exchange information
  - Debate/promote policy, especially 'big-ticket' items
- Cabinet officers may see meetings as a chance
  - to get to know colleagues
  - to resolve interdepartmental disputes
  - for manual praise and congratulation (Trump)
  - to speak to the president

Remember

The following comment is the kind of scholarly quotation that you should aim to use in your essays:

'The cabinet has become institutionalised by usage alone' (Richard Fenno). In other words, it's used because it's used.

Compare

Cabinet ministers in the UK come from a much narrower range of places than US cabinet officers. Which institution are cabinet ministers most likely to come from? Can they stay members of this institution?

Remember

Don't use the term 'cabinet ministers' when discussing the USA. The correct term is 'cabinet officers'.

Compare

Unlike in the USA, UK cabinet meetings are held on a regular basis. How often does the UK prime minister hold cabinet meetings? What does this indicate about the importance of the cabinet to the UK executive, in comparison to the USA?

Debate

Is the president's cabinet important?

Yes	No
+ It contains some of the most important people in the executive branch (e.g. secretary of state, secretary of defense). + All the heads of the 15 executive departments are automatically members + The president always chairs the meetings. + Cabinet meetings can fulfil a number of important functions, both for the president and for cabinet officers. + Some presidents hold frequent meetings (e.g. Reagan).	+ Article II of the Constitution vests 'all executive power' in the president. + There is no doctrine of collective responsibility. + The members are neither the president's equals nor political rivals. + Presidents often view members of their cabinet with some suspicion because of their divided loyalties. + EXOP is the main source of advice-giving for the president.

Revision activity

Draw up a table showing the differences between collective and individual ministerial responsibility. Add examples of both from your knowledge of UK politics.

Now test yourself

TESTED 

8 Give a definition of the president's cabinet.
9 Why do so few cabinet members come from Congress?

Remember

When debating the importance of the cabinet, you may need to distinguish between the cabinet as a group (i.e. the cabinet meeting) and cabinet officers as individuals.

10 Where else do presidents look when recruiting their cabinet?
11 In what ways do presidents seek to appoint a balanced cabinet?
12 What functions can cabinet meetings serve for the president?
13 What functions can cabinet meetings serve for cabinet members?

Answers on p. 114

Remember

Be prepared to answer a question on how effective and important the president's cabinet is. Even if this question is not in the comparative section of the exam paper, it would be useful to include a comparison with the prime minister's cabinet, as there are significant differences between the two.

The Executive Office of the President

REVISED

The Executive Office of the President (EXOP) was established in 1939 with just four offices.

- By 2020 EXOP was made up of 13 offices.
- The number has increased because the number of policy areas that the president must address has increased.
- Key EXOP personnel work in the West Wing (where the Oval Office is located).
- The three most important offices within the Executive Office of the President are the White House Office (WHO), the Office of Management and Budget (OMB) and the National Security Council (NSC).

Executive Office of the President (EXOP) The umbrella term for the top staff agencies in the White House that assist the president in carrying out the major responsibilities of office.

Remember

EXOP is not an office alongside the White House Office, OMB, NSC, etc. It is the umbrella organisation that is **made up** of the White House Office, OMB, NSC, etc.

White House Office (WHO)

Also known as the White House Staff, this includes the president's most trusted aides and advisers.

It is made up of more than 30 different offices, such as:

- Office of Legislative Affairs
- Office of Cabinet Affairs

It acts as liaison between the White House and the vast federal bureaucracy.

- Staff are meant to act as neutral 'honest brokers', not partisan policy-makers.
- It is headed by the White House chief of staff:
  - The door-keeper of the Oval Office
  - Decides whom the president sees, what the president reads, who speaks to the president on the phone
  - Should act as someone who sometimes takes the blame for the president if things go wrong
  - All of Trump's four chiefs of staff struggled to fulfil these roles, given Trump's way of operating
  - Potentially the most powerful person in the White House after the president

Office of Management and Budget (OMB)

The OMB is headed by the OMB director.

- The appointment requires Senate confirmation.
- The OMB has three principal functions:
  - To advise the president on the allocation of federal funds in the annual budget
  - To oversee the spending of all federal departments and agencies
  - To act as a clearing house for all legislative and regulatory initiatives coming from the president

National Security Council (NSC)

The main function of the NSC is to help the president coordinate foreign, security and defence policy.

- It is headed by the national security adviser.
- The NSC coordinates information coming to the president from:
  - the State Department
  - the Defense Department
  - the Central Intelligence Agency (CIA)
  - the joint chiefs of staff
  - US ambassadors around the world
- It is important that the NSC acts as an 'honest broker', a facilitator, not a policy promoter.

Remember

When revising, use an internet search engine to find out something that one of these three offices within EXOP has been recently involved in. It's good example material!

The problem of EXOP–cabinet rivalries

In many administrations, rivalries break out between those who work in EXOP and those who work in the cabinet. Rivalries can develop for various reasons:

- While EXOP members work in or near the West Wing, cabinet members often work some geographic distance from the White House.
- While key EXOP members may see the president on a regular basis, some members of the cabinet rarely get to see the president — and certainly not one on one.
- Therefore, while EXOP members often know what the president wants from day to day, cabinet members may feel out of the loop.
- While EXOP members work only for the president, cabinet members have divided loyalties — to the president, but also to Congress, to their bureaucracy and to client interest groups.
- EXOP staff therefore often regard cabinet members as being disloyal.

Compare

The UK prime minister does not have an 'executive office' but that does not mean that he or she doesn't have their own team of advisers. What is the prime minister's group of advisers often known as? What rivalries, if any, do you think they have with the cabinet?

Now test yourself TESTED

14 What is the Executive Office of the President (EXOP)?

15 How many offices made up EXOP in 2020?

16 What is the main function of the White House Office?

17 Give three key roles of the White House chief of staff.

18 Give two functions of the Office of Management and Budget (OMB).

19 What is the main function of the National Security Council (NSC)?

20 Name three organisations/groups of people from whom the NSC coordinates information.

21 Give three reasons why rivalries can develop between EXOP and members of the president's cabinet.

Answers on pp. 114–15

The powers of persuasion

REVISED

This is an informal power of the president in which they can use the prestige of their job and other bargaining methods to get people to do as they wish. In the modern era of party polarisation, the president's powers of persuasion are less effective than they were in the postwar period when bipartisan politics was more common.

A president's power to persuade is usually greater when there is unified government.

Unified government When both houses of Congress and the presidency are controlled by the same party.

Remember

If you are answering a question about how the president persuades/works with members of Congress, make sure you begin your answer by explaining why the president needs their support.

The president's relations with Congress

What is the president trying to get Congress to do?

- Pass the president's legislative proposals.
- Sustain the president's vetoes.
- Confirm the president's executive and judicial nominations (Senate only).
- Ratify the president's treaties (Senate only).

Why does a president need to persuade Congress to give its support?

- The president's powers are checked by Congress (see Table 3.4).
- The president's party may control only one house of Congress, or neither.
- Members of Congress have other loyalties than to the president, especially to their constituents and to powerful lobbyists.
- Members of Congress are elected separately from the president.
- The president has few 'sticks and carrots' (disincentives and incentives) to encourage members of Congress to offer their support.

Table 3.4 Powers of the president and checks by Congress

Powers of the president	Checks by Congress
Propose legislation	Amend, delay, reject the president's legislative proposals
Veto legislation	Override the veto
Nominate executive branch officials	Senate has the power to confirm or reject
Nominate federal judges	Senate has the power to confirm or reject
Negotiate treaties	Senate has the power to ratify or reject
Commander-in-chief of the armed forces	Declare war/power of the purse
Act as chief executive	Investigation, impeachment, trial, removal from office

Remember

Make sure that you know at least one example of each of the powers and checks listed in Table 3.4, so that you can provide substance to any answer you write about the president's powers.

Whom does the president use to help get Congress's support?

- The vice president
- The Office of Legislative Affairs (part of the White House Office)
- Cabinet officers
- Party leadership in Congress

What 'perks' can the president use to help win the support of members of Congress?

- Phone calls to members of Congress to request their support directly
- Support legislation important to a member of Congress
- Invitations — social or political — to the White House
- Campaign for them (only for members from the president's party)
- Go on TV to appeal directly to voters and ask them to contact their members of Congress and tell them to support the president

What success have recent presidents enjoyed in Congress?

- Success can be measured by the presidential support score — an annual statistic that measures how often the president won in recorded votes in Congress on which the president took a clear position, expressed as a percentage of all such votes

- Figure 3.1 shows that President Obama's support score varied from 97% in 2009 to just 39% in 2016.
- A president's support score tends to be higher earlier in their presidency, and also when their party controls both houses of Congress — as Obama's Democrats did in 2009 and 2010.

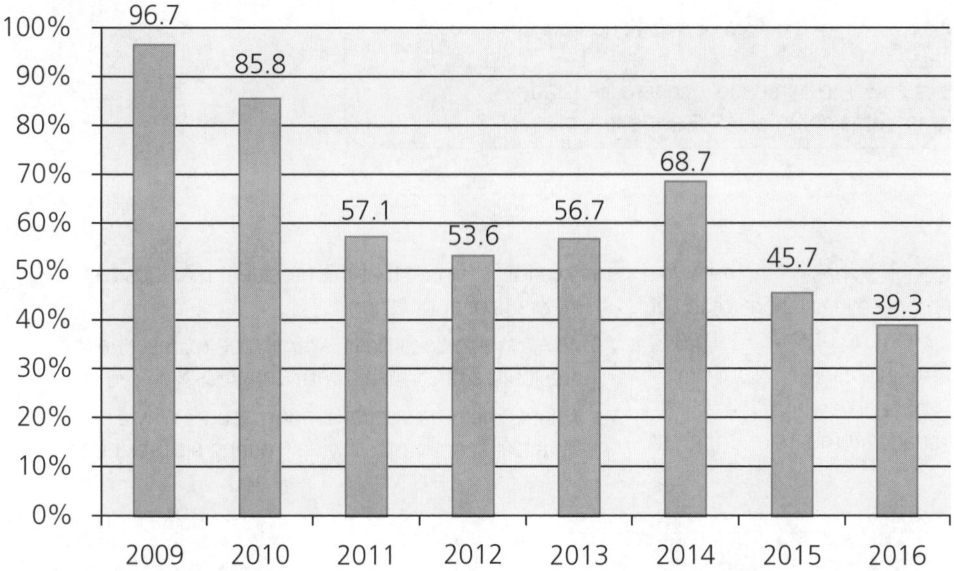

Figure 3.1 President Obama's presidential support score, 2009–16

The changing nature of power over their term in office

In their second terms, presidents can quickly become 'lame ducks'. The average first-year presidential support score for presidents from Reagan to Obama is 83%, while the average last-year score is around 48%.

George W. Bush's approval rating averaged 62% during his first term but just 37% during his second. Barack Obama's highest approval rating during his presidency was 67%, recorded during his first week in office in 2009. His low point was 40%, just after his second midterm elections in 2014. This is why presidents always try to enact their top policy priorities early in their first term when they are usually most popular.

President Trump's approval score during his four years in office ranged from 47% at its highest in October 2018 to 34% at its lowest in January 2021 at the end of his term.

Debate

Is the president's power of persuasion still important?

Yes	No
+ The president has no formal disciplinary hold over members of Congress. + Party discipline in Congress, though tighter than it used to be, cannot guarantee votes for the president. + The president may be faced with one or both houses of Congress controlled by the other party. + The president is dependent upon members of Congress for legislation, confirmation of appointments and treaty ratification. + The president's 'direct authority' (see page 48) has limited use. + The president can offer support for things members of Congress regard as important.	+ In an era of partisanship, few (if any) members of Congress from the opposition party are open to presidential persuasion, especially on big-ticket items. + Partisanship also makes persuasion a less useful tool for the president trying to persuade voters to support him and then pressurise recalcitrant members of Congress to do likewise. + Presidents nowadays tend to have low approval ratings (and high disapproval ratings) and therefore their persuasion is much less effective. + Second-term presidents have often found their persuasive power to be very limited.

Remember

Some quotations to use in your essays about the relations between the president and Congress include:

- The president and Congress are part of a system of 'separated institutions, sharing powers' (Richard Neustadt).
- The president and Congress are like 'two halves of a bank note, each useless without the other' (S.E. Finer).
- 'The president's power is the power to persuade' (Richard Neustadt).
- The president needs to act as 'bargainer-in-chief' (David Mervin).

Now test yourself

TESTED

22 What are the checks that Congress has on the following presidential powers: (a) to propose legislation; (b) to veto legislation; (c) to nominate executive officials and federal judges; (d) to negotiate treaties?

23 Name three people/groups of people whom the president might use to persuade members of Congress to give their support.

24 Give three 'perks' that the president might use as methods of persuasion.

25 What phrase does David Mervin use to describe the president's relationship with Congress?

26 What is the presidential support score? Why did Obama's score vary so widely during his presidency?

Answers on p. 115

Direct authority

REVISED

Frustrated by the checks imposed upon them as well as by the partisan gridlock in Washington, presidents have made increasing use of what is called direct authority — actions they can take which do not require congressional approval and yet can achieve some of their policy goals.

You need to be familiar with four types of direct authority.

Executive orders

- An executive order is easy for a president to issue, but equally easy for a subsequent president to rescind.
- Obama made increasing use of them after the Democrats lost control of Congress.
- Trump made significant use of them during his first few months, also facing an uncooperative Congress.

Signing statements

- George W. Bush increasingly used signing statements to challenge the constitutionality of some part of a bill he was signing.
- Critics claim they are an abuse of presidential power over legislation — that the correct and constitutional course of action would be for the president either to veto the bill, or to await a ruling on the law's constitutionality from the Supreme Court.
- Supporters see them as a way in which a president can get their way over legislation even when Congress is uncooperative.

Recess appointments

- A recess appointment is another way of the president getting their way against an uncooperative Congress — this time gridlock in the Senate over confirmation of appointments.
- Bill Clinton and George W. Bush increasingly used them over their terms in office.
- Barack Obama lost a Supreme Court decision about them in 2014, which resulted in their curtailment.

Executive order An official document issued by the executive branch with the effect of law, through which the president directs federal officials to take certain actions.

Signing statement A statement issued by the president on signing a bill which may challenge specific provisions of the bill on constitutional or other grounds.

Recess appointment A temporary appointment of a federal official made by the president to fill a vacancy while the Senate is in recess.

Executive agreements

- The president uses executive agreements to circumvent the Senate's power to ratify treaties.
- Hence there is strong opposition to them from Congress.

Executive agreement An agreement reached between the president and a foreign nation on matters that do not require a formal treaty.

Now test yourself TESTED

27 What is an executive order?
28 Why do presidents tend to use them?
29 What is a signing statement?
30 What are their pros and cons?
31 What is a recess appointment?
32 Why have presidents used them?

Answers on p. 115

Theories of presidential power

Three theories of presidential power are explained in Table 3.5. Table 3.6 gives some examples of the ways in which critics have argued that different presidents have acted as imperial presidents.

Table 3.5 Theories of presidential power

Imperial presidency	+ Term first used by Arthur Schlesinger (1973) + Associated most with President Nixon (1969–74) + Characterised by abuse of power, secrecy (especially within the White House) and illegality
Imperilled presidency	+ Term first used by Gerald Ford (1980) + Associated most with presidents Ford (1974–77) and Carter (1977–81) + Characterised by congressional re-assertiveness and presidential weakness
Post-imperial presidency	+ Term first used in 1980 + Often used to refer to presidents from Reagan to Trump + Characterised by presidential re-assertiveness but power that is often limited by a new era of hyper-partisanship

Table 3.6 Ways in which presidents since 1992 have acted in an imperial manner

Bill Clinton	+ In 1994 Clinton was prepared to launch an invasion of Haiti without congressional permission. + In the March–June 1999 Serbian air war, the USA committed the most US personnel since the Gulf War, without a declaration of war from Congress. + Sanctioning missile strikes on Sudan and Afghanistan (for links to terrorism) as a distraction from the Lewinsky affair.
George W. Bush	+ Bush's unilateralism accelerated dramatically after the events of 9/11.
Barack Obama	+ A major offensive was launched in Afghanistan in 2010 and Obama signed a four-year extension to Bush's Patriot Act. + Obama launched ten times as many airstrikes in the Middle East and Asia as George W. Bush; likewise he sanctioned a military intervention in Libya without seeking congressional approval. + Most controversially, he sanctioned the death of Anwar al-Awlaki, an alleged terrorist, by a drone attack in Yemen in 2011.
Donald Trump	+ Pulling the USA out of the Iran nuclear deal, the North American Free Trade Agreement, and the Paris Accord. + Bombing ISIS fighters in April 2017. + The airstrike assassination of Iranian general Qasem Soleimani in January 2020 without authorisation or consultation with Congress. + Argued in January 2020 that he could use Twitter to inform Congress of future airstrikes.

Remember

When discussing presidential 'power', you need to be clear about the difference between 'powers' (the tasks of the office), which are the same for each president, and 'power' (the ability to get things done), which varies between presidents and even within a presidency.

Imperial presidency A presidency characterised by the misuse of presidential powers, especially excessive secrecy — particularly in foreign policy — and high-handedness in dealing with Congress.

Imperilled presidency A term coined by President Gerald Ford to refer to a presidency characterised by ineffectiveness and weakness, resulting from congressional over-assertiveness.

Now test yourself TESTED

33 Give a definition of the imperial presidency. With which president was it particularly associated?
34 Give a definition of the imperilled presidency. With which two presidents was it particularly associated?
35 What is the main characteristic of the post-imperial presidency?

Answers on p. 115

The president and foreign policy

The Constitution gives the president certain powers in foreign policy:

- To act as commander-in-chief of the armed forces
- To negotiate treaties with foreign powers
- To make certain appointments (e.g. secretary of state, secretary of defense, director of the CIA, ambassadors)

But the Constitution also gives Congress certain powers in foreign policy:

- To declare war (but not used since 1941)
- Control of the budget (including military spending)
- To ratify treaties (Senate only)
- To confirm appointments (Senate only)
- To investigate (through such committees as the Senate Foreign Relations Committee, and the House Armed Services Committee)

The control of foreign policy is therefore often seen as a struggle between the president and Congress.

Remember

When discussing Congress's power to declare war, be clear that only a simple majority is needed in both houses to do this. Always mention that the power was last used in 1941.

Making links

It is the checks and balances written into the US Constitution which determine these powers.

Debate

Does the president control foreign policy?

Yes	No
+ The president is commander-in-chief. + The president has the power to negotiate treaties. + The president has the power to make appointments. + The president can set the tone of foreign policy. + The president has access to the nuclear 'button' ('the football'). + The president 'has the facts' in a crisis.	+ Congress controls the purse strings. + Only Congress can declare war (though this is largely redundant now). + The Senate has ratification power for treaties. + The Senate has confirmation power of appointments. + Congress has the power of investigation.

Compare

In the UK, the question of whether the prime minister can declare war is controversial. Who is ultimately responsible for declaring war — the monarch, Parliament or the prime minister?

Now test yourself 

36 Name the three powers related to foreign policy that the Constitution gives to the president.
37 Name three powers related to foreign policy that the Constitution gives to Congress.

Answers on p. 115

Limits on presidential power

Presidents face numerous checks on their power — from Congress, from the Supreme Court and from other sources, too (see Table 3.7).

Table 3.7 Checks on the president's power

Source	Checks
Congress	+ Amend, delay, reject the president's legislative proposals and budgetary requests + Override the president's veto + Refuse to ratify treaties (Senate) + Refuse to confirm appointments (Senate) + Investigate the president's actions and policies + Impeach, try and remove the president from office
Supreme Court	+ Declare the president's actions to be unconstitutional (for more details, see Chapter 4)
Interest groups	+ Mobilise public opinion against the president's policy proposals
Public opinion	+ Low approval ratings give the president less political clout
Voters	+ In special and midterm elections, as well as in re-election bid
Federal bureaucracy	+ Federal departments/agencies may frustrate the president's wishes
State governments	+ Presidents often rely upon state governments to enact presidential policies

Compare

UK prime ministers also have constraints on their power. Construct a similar table to Table 3.7 detailing the extent of accountability of the UK prime minister.

In practice, presidential success is limited by several other factors, which vary between presidents (see Table 3.8). An assessment of how effective recent presidents have been in achieving their aims is given in Table 3.9.

Table 3.8 Factors affecting presidential success and how they vary between presidents

Electoral mandate	+ The electoral mandate is the percentage of popular vote won in the previous election. + Note the difference between Obama winning 52.9% (2008) and Trump winning 46% (2016). + Bush (2000) and Trump (2016) both lost the popular vote.
Public approval	+ The higher the president's public approval rating, the more political clout they are likely to have. + Note the difference between George W. Bush (62% approval average in first year) and Donald Trump (38% approval average in first year).
First/second term	+ The president is likely to be more successful in the first two years of their first term than in the last two years of their second term. + George W. Bush had an approval rating of 62% during his first term and only 37% during his second term; Obama had a rating of 67% in his first term, falling to 40% in his second term.
Unified/divided government	+ They are likely to be more successful if their party controls both houses of Congress. + For example, Clinton 1993–95 and Obama 2009–11.
Crises	+ In a crisis, the nation tends to 'rally round the flag' and look to the president for leadership. + But if the president is seen to mishandle the crisis, it can have the opposite effect (e.g. Trump and the Covid-19 pandemic).

Table 3.9 How effectively have presidents achieved their aims?

President	Aim	Effectiveness
Bill Clinton	Economic growth	The economic recovery of the 1990s led to his presidency being remembered for a booming economy.
	Affordable healthcare	His proposed healthcare reforms were too divisive in Congress and ended up not even being voted on.
	Expanding civil rights	Successfully increased representation of ethnic groups and women in government during his presidency and had some success in advancing gay rights in the military.
	Foreign policy	Clinton was successful in his foreign policy in both Russia and Yugoslavia as well as playing a crucial part in negotiating an end to 'The Troubles' in Northern Ireland.
George W. Bush	'War on terror' post 9/11	Bush was successful in creating a homeland security department that increased mass surveillance to prevent another attack of the magnitude of 9/11.
	Education reform	The 'No Child Left Behind' policy saw a 2% increase in spending for inner-city schools and the most vulnerable children in US society.
	Major tax cuts	Succeeded in his aim of making $1.35 trillion worth of tax cuts.
	Social security reform	Bush underestimated the difficulties he would face in passing his bill, taking the support of Congress for granted. His reform was not acted upon by Congress.
Barack Obama	Healthcare reform	Passing healthcare reform was a considerable achievement. Obamacare saw the number of adults uninsured for healthcare drop considerably.
	Stimulating the economy	He successfully saw the USA through the 2008 economic crisis, with Congress passing two major pieces of legislation essential to his plans: the American Recovery and Reinvestment Act (2009) and the Dodd–Frank Wall Street Reform Consumer Protection Act (2019).
	Ending the war in Iraq	The Obama administration was successful in engineering an exit strategy that ended the war in Iraq.
	Immigration reform	Obama failed to achieve an immigration reform which he hoped would lead to citizenship for the children of illegal immigrants. He underestimated the opposition within his own party to the reforms. Likewise, his attempt to bypass Congress and extend the rights of illegal immigrants via executive order was eventually ruled unconstitutional by the Supreme Court in the *United States* v *Texas* (2016) ruling.
Donald Trump	Taxes and jobs	The Tax and Jobs Act (2017) was the biggest overhaul in the nation's tax codes for 30 years, slashing the corporate tax rate from 35% to 21%. In September 2019, the US economy saw the unemployment rate fall to its lowest level since 1969.
	Immigration	Policy agreements with Central American countries were successful in reducing the number of migrants illegally trying to enter the USA.
	Repeal and replace Obamacare	The Trump administration lacked a clear vision of what the replacement for Obamacare would look like and this lack of clarity resulted in a Republican Senate failing to back the administration's plans. Trump underestimated the difficulty of passing healthcare reform.
	'Build the Wall'	Trump failed to build a wall across the USA–Mexico border. He claimed to have built around 450 miles of wall, but at least 350 miles of this replaced wall that already existed.
	Successfully manage the Covid-19 crisis	The Trump administration was slow to recognise the danger of the virus and failed to communicate a national response. The USA was the worst-affected country in the world in terms of total fatalities.

Now test yourself TESTED

38 Name three checks that Congress has on presidential power.

39 What check does the Supreme Court have on presidential power?

40 Name three other groups/institutions that can check presidential power.

41 Name three factors that can affect presidential success.

42 What effect can crises have on presidential success?

Answers on p. 115

Comparing the president with the UK prime minister

Structural differences

REVISED

There are important structural differences which one must always keep in mind whenever comparing or contrasting these two offices (see Table 3.10).

Table 3.10 Structural differences between the offices of US president and UK prime minister

US president	UK prime minister
The presidency is a product of revolution — the War of Independence (1776–83)	The office of the UK prime minister is a product of evolution over centuries
The president is elected as president by the people (through the Electoral College)	The prime minister is elected as party leader by the party
The president is entirely separate from the legislature	The prime minister is part of the legislature
The president is limited to two terms	There are no term limits
The president is aided by an advisory cabinet	The cabinet is more than just an advisory body
The president may be removed only by impeachment	The prime minister may be removed by a leadership vote in the party or as a consequence of losing a vote of confidence in the House of Commons

Comparing roles and powers

REVISED

Being part of a singular executive, the US president has more in the way of roles and powers than does the UK prime minister, who is part of a plural executive working within a doctrine of collective responsibility (see Table 3.11). These significant differences in their roles and powers can largely be attributed to the structural differences listed in Table 3.10.

Table 3.11 Roles and powers compared

US president	UK prime minister
Fulfils roles of both head of state and chief executive	Fulfils only chief executive role (the monarch is head of state)
Has formal input only at the start and finish of the legislative process: initiating and signing/vetoing powers	Draws up government's legislative programme with the cabinet; has no veto power
Appoints cabinet, subject to Senate confirmation	Appoints cabinet (no confirmation required)
Commander-in-chief of the armed forces, but only Congress can declare war (though it has not done so since 1941)	Can use the royal prerogative to declare war and deploy troops abroad, but recently this has been subject to parliamentary approval
Has an elected vice president who automatically succeeds if the president dies, resigns or is removed from office	May appoint an unofficial deputy prime minister
Has (large) Executive Office of the President	Has (small) Number 10 staff and Cabinet Office
Has a variety of powers to pursue policy unilaterally: executive orders, signing statements, executive agreements	More likely to pursue policy collectively, through either the full cabinet or cabinet committees
Submits annual budget to Congress, which is then subject to months of negotiation and numerous changes	Submits annual budget to Parliament, which is debated but usually passed without any significant amendment
Appoints all federal judges	Does not appoint judges (this is done by the Judicial Appointments Commission)
Has power of pardon and commutation of prison sentences	Has no pardon power (only the monarch can grant a pardon)

Comparing relations with the legislature

When comparing the president and the UK prime minister in their relations with their respective legislatures (see Table 3.12), remember the following:

- Whereas the president is entirely separate from Congress, the UK prime minister is not only a member of the House of Commons but also the leader of the largest party in that chamber and, as such, virtually controls its business and legislative outcomes.
- Whereas the president cannot be questioned by members of Congress — although members of the administration can be called before committees — the UK prime minister and their ministerial team are under constant scrutiny by Parliament.

Table 3.12 Levels of accountability to the legislature compared

US president's relations with Congress	UK prime minister's relations with Parliament
Not a serving member of Congress; must resign if serving when elected (e.g. Obama)	Serving member of Parliament
No executive branch members permitted to be serving members of Congress	Cabinet and government ministers are serving members of Parliament
Not subject to personal questioning by members of Congress	Weekly Prime Minister's Questions (when House of Commons is sitting)
Legislative agenda often introduced in annual State of the Union Address	Legislative programme introduced in annual Queen's Speech
Gets agreement in Congress mostly by persuasion and bargaining	Gets agreement in Parliament mostly by party discipline and reliance on the payroll vote
Dependent on Senate confirmation for numerous appointments	Makes numerous appointments without the need for consent by Parliament
President's party may control only one chamber of Congress, or neither	Prime minister's party controls the House of Commons but may not have a majority in the House of Lords

Comparing cabinets

REVISED

It is tempting to say that the only similarity between the US and UK cabinets is their name. Structural differences between the two governmental systems are again at the root of the significant differences (see Table 3.13).

Table 3.13 Significant differences between the US and the UK cabinets

US cabinet	UK cabinet
Serving members of the legislature barred from serving	Membership exclusive to Members of Parliament
Presidential appointments to the cabinet subject to Senate confirmation (though rarely rejected)	No formal limits on cabinet appointments
President decides frequency and regularity of meetings	Prime minister obliged to maintain frequency and regularity of meetings
Cabinet members are subordinate to the president, who is in no way 'first among equals'; cabinet does not take decisions — the president does	Cabinet is a collective decision-making body, at least in theory. The prime minister is considered to be 'first among equals' within the cabinet
Cabinet members recruited mostly for their policy specialisation; rarely moved to a different department	Cabinet members are usually policy generalists; hence cabinet reshuffles
Cabinet members are often strangers to the president (and sometimes to each other); no shadow cabinet	Cabinet is made up of long-serving parliamentary colleagues and former shadow cabinet members
Cabinet meetings are often the only time some cabinet members see the president	Prime minister sees cabinet colleagues regularly in Parliament
No doctrine of collective responsibility	Collective responsibility usually applies

Now test yourself TESTED

43 Give four structural differences between the offices of the US president and the UK prime minister.

44 Give four ways in which these two offices are different in terms of their roles and powers.

45 What basic reason accounts for the different relations that the US president and the UK prime minister have with their respective legislatures?

46 Why does the author suggest that 'the only similarity between the US and UK cabinets is their name'?

Answers on pp. 115–16

Using comparative approaches when comparing the US president with the UK prime minister

REVISED

Table 3.14 shows how the three comparative approaches can be used when comparing different elements of the US presidency and the office of UK prime minister.

Table 3.14 Comparative approaches to comparing the US president and UK prime minister

Topic	Rational approach	Cultural approach	Structural approach
Character	Elections for presidency are usually focused on the individual.	The presidency is a product of revolution whereas the office of prime minister has evolved over centuries.	The president is directly elected whereas the prime minister is the leader of the winning political party.
Roles and powers		The president is both head of state and chief executive (head of government). In the UK the monarch is the head of state.	
Relations with the legislature	The president gets agreement in Congress mainly through persuasion and bargaining.		The prime minister is a member of the legislature whereas in the USA the separation of powers principle prevents this. The prime minister's party controls the House of Commons whereas in the USA there might be divided government.
Comparing cabinets		UK cabinets usually abide by the collective responsibility principle, which does not exist in the USA.	Members of the UK cabinet must be Members of Parliament.

Summary

You should now have an understanding of:

- the powers of the president — both formal and informal
- the vice president
- the president's cabinet
- the Executive Office of the President
- the president's relations with Congress
- the president's use of direct authority
- theories of presidential power
- the role of the president in foreign policy
- limitations on presidential power
- factors that affect presidential success
- how effectively different presidents have achieved their aims
- the similarities and differences between the US president and the UK prime minister
- using comparative approaches to compare presidents and prime ministers

Exam practice

Section A (comparative)

1 Examine the ways in which the roles and powers of the US president and the UK prime minister are different. [12]

2 Examine the differences in the relationship that the US president and the UK prime minister have with their respective legislatures. [12]

Section B (comparative)

In your answer you must consider the relevance of at least one comparative theory.

3 Analyse the different ways in which the US president and the UK prime minister appoint their cabinets. [12]

4 Analyse the different ways in which the US president and the UK prime minister are held accountable by their respective legislatures. [12]

Section C (USA)

In your answer you must consider this view and the alternative to this view in a balanced way.

5 Evaluate the extent to which the president is subject to effective checks. [30]

6 Evaluate the extent to which the president's cabinet plays a significant role within the executive branch. [30]

7 Evaluate the view that Congress dominates US foreign policy as much as the presidency. [30]

Answers and quick quiz online

4 The Supreme Court

The Supreme Court sits atop the federal judiciary.

Below the Supreme Court are the US courts of appeal (also known as circuit courts) and the US district courts (also known as trial courts).

Membership of the Supreme Court

- The Court consists of nine justices (one chief justice and eight associate justices).
- These are nominated by the president.
- Their appointment needs to be confirmed by a simple majority of the Senate.
- Justices are appointed for life.
- Justices usually leave service by voluntary resignation (retirement) or on dying. If necessary, they can be impeached and, if found guilty, removed from office.
- Anthony Kennedy, appointed by Ronald Reagan in 1987, served for more than 30 years on the bench before his recent retirement.
- Chief Justice at the time of writing is John Roberts (appointed by George W. Bush in 2005).
- Newest member at the time of writing is Amy Coney Barrett (appointed by Donald Trump in 2020).

Compare

The Supreme Court in the UK is much less established than the US Supreme Court, only having been founded in 2009. Although its creation was influenced by the more famous US Supreme Court, it doesn't have as much power as its US counterpart. How many members does the UK Supreme Court have?

Now test yourself TESTED

1 How many justices make up the Supreme Court?
2 Who nominates them?
3 How are they confirmed?
4 How long do they serve?
5 What are the only ways justices leave the Court?

Answers on p. 116

Judicial philosophy

There are two main strands of judicial philosophy with which you need to be familiar, shown in Table 4.1. Details of the composition of the current Supreme Court and the justices' judicial philosophies are provided in Table 4.2.

Table 4.1 The two main strands of judicial philosophy

Strict constructionists/ originalists	**Originalism** tends to: + interpret the Constitution in a strict, literal fashion + favour state government rights over federal government power + lead to an outcome that is often seen as being 'conservative' + try to interpret the Constitution in line with its original meaning and intent (hence 'originalists') + be appointed by Republican presidents (e.g. John Roberts, strict constructionist; Antonin Scalia, originalist)
Loose constructionists/ living Constitution	Loose constructionists tend to: + interpret the Constitution in a loose fashion + favour federal government power over state government rights + read elements into the document that they think the framers would have approved of + see the Constitution as a living, dynamic document, which should be adapted to take account of the views of contemporary society (hence 'living Constitution') + be seen as **liberal justices** + be appointed by Democratic presidents (e.g. Sonia Sotomayor, Elena Kagan)

Table 4.2 Supreme Court justices and their judicial philosophies, 2021

Loose constructionists	Strict constructionists
Stephen Breyer (Clinton)	John Roberts (George W. Bush) (swing justice?)
Sonia Sotomayor (Obama)	Clarence Thomas (George H.W. Bush)
Elena Kagan (Obama)	Samuel Alito (George W. Bush)
	Neil Gorsuch (Trump)
	Brett Kavanaugh (Trump)
	Amy Coney Barrett (Trump)

Sometimes a justice can be described as a **swing justice**. Justice Anthony Kennedy played this role, especially between 2005 and his retirement in 2018. Chief Justice Roberts has shown a tendency to play the role in some high-profile cases: for example, *Bostock* v *Clayton County, Georgia* (2020) on LGBTQ+ rights; *Department of Homeland Security* v *University of California* (2020) on DACA beneficiaries; and *June Medical Services* v *Russo* (2020) on abortion rights.

Now test yourself TESTED

6 What is the difference between strict and loose constructionists?

Remember

Strict construction and loose construction are technical, legal terms. Think of the word 'construction' as meaning 'interpretation'.

7 Give an example of each from the current Court.
8 How would you classify former justice Anthony Kennedy?
9 What does the term 'originalist' mean?
10 If a justice believes in a 'living Constitution', what does that mean?

Answers on p. 116

Strict constructionist A Supreme Court justice who interprets the Constitution strictly or literally and tends to stress the retention of power by individual states.

Originalism Where a Supreme Court justice interprets the Constitution in line with the meaning or intent of the framers at the time of enactment.

Loose constructionist A Supreme Court justice who interprets the Constitution less literally and tends to stress the broad grants of power to the federal government.

Living Constitution The Constitution considered as a dynamic, living document, interpretation of which should take account of the views of contemporary society.

Liberal justice A Supreme Court justice who is usually a loose constructionist and generally interprets the Constitution in ways that give people more freedom.

Swing justice The pivotal justice in an otherwise evenly balanced Court, who will often be in a position of casting the deciding vote.

The appointment and confirmation process

The appointment of Supreme Court justices is a five-stage process:

1 A vacancy occurs.
2 The president instigates a search for possible nominees and interviews shortlisted candidates.
3 The president announces their nominee.
4 The Senate Judiciary Committee holds confirmation hearings on the nominee and makes a recommendatory vote.
5 The nomination is debated and voted on in the full Senate. A simple majority vote is required for confirmation.

See Table 4.3 for an example of a Supreme Court nomination timeline.

Compare

While similar to the US Supreme Court, the process of appointing a Supreme Court justice in the UK does differ. Construct a list similar to that in Table 4.3 to illustrate the process of appointing a UK Supreme Court justice.

Table 4.3 Timeline of Supreme Court nomination, 2018

28 June	Associate Justice Anthony Kennedy announces his retirement.
2 July	President Trump conducts personal interviews with four federal judges he is considering for nomination to the Supreme Court.
9 July	President Trump nominates Judge Brett Kavanaugh to fill the vacancy.
4 September	Senate Judiciary Committee begins hearings on Kavanaugh nomination.
28 September	Senate Judiciary Committee votes 11–10 in favour of recommending Kavanaugh's confirmation.
6 October	Senate votes 50–48 to confirm Kavanaugh to the Supreme Court.
7 October	Brett Kavanaugh sworn in as associate justice of the Supreme Court.

When appointing a new Supreme Court justice, the factors affecting the president's choice of nominee include whether the nominee:

- shares a similar judicial philosophy to the president
- is quite young — meaning they are likely to remain on the Court for longer
- is likely to be acceptable to a majority of the Senate (especially important if the president's party is in the minority)
- has an uncontroversial background — from both a judicial and a personal point of view
- is going to be highly rated professionally (by the American Bar Association)
- has relevant experience

Remember

The vote in the Senate Judiciary Committee is only a recommendatory vote. The final decision is made by the full Senate — even if the nominee were to lose the committee vote.

The confirmation process has changed over recent years:

- Supreme Court nominees used to be approved mostly by overwhelming, bipartisan votes (e.g. Anthony Kennedy, 97–0 in 1988).
- Nowadays, although rejections are still rare, confirmation votes are much more likely to be along party lines, with pretty much all the senators from the president's party voting 'yes' and those from the other party voting 'no' (e.g. Brett Kavanaugh, 50–48 in 2018 — with 49 Republicans plus 1 Democrat voting 'yes', 48 Democrats voting 'no').

Remember

Never refer to nominees or justices as being 'Democrats' or 'Republicans'.

There are some significant criticisms of the appointment and confirmation process:

- Presidents have tended to politicise the nominations by attempting to choose justices who share their political views and judicial philosophy (e.g. Obama with Kagan; Trump with Gorsuch, Kavanaugh and Coney Barrett).
- The Senate has tended to politicise the confirmation process by focusing more on hot-button issues (e.g. women's rights) than on qualifications.
- Members of the Senate Judiciary Committee from the president's party tend to ask soft questions of the nominee.
- Members of the Senate Judiciary Committee from the opposition party attempt, through their questions, to attack or embarrass the nominee rather than to elicit relevant information.

- Justices are now frequently confirmed on party-line votes (e.g. Kavanaugh).
- The media conduct a 'feeding frenzy' often connected with matters of trivia.

It is often said that these are the most important nominations a president makes because:

- they occur infrequently
- they are for life
- just one new appointee to a nine-member body can significantly change its philosophical balance
- the Supreme Court has the power of judicial review
- their decisions will profoundly affect the lives of ordinary Americans for generations to come

Now test yourself TESTED 

11 What are the five stages of the appointment and confirmation process?
12 What has changed in the way the Senate now votes on Supreme Court nominees?
13 Identify three significant criticisms of the appointment and confirmation process.
14 Give three reasons why these nominations are said to be the most important a president makes.

Answers on p. 116

The power of judicial review

- The power of judicial review is not mentioned in the Constitution.
- It was 'found' by the Court in *Marbury* v *Madison* (1803) — regarding a federal law.
- It was used again in *Fletcher* v *Peck* (1810) — regarding a state law.
- It has been used since then in a host of cases to guarantee fundamental civil rights and liberties.
- Hence the Court's political importance because it rules on key political issues such as the rights of racial minorities, capital punishment, gun control and freedom of speech.
- This turns the Court into a quasi-legislative body — because the effects of its decisions have almost the effect of a law having been passed by Congress.
- For example, *Roe* v *Wade* (1973) had the effect comparable to an abortion rights law having been passed by Congress.
- It turns the Court into a 'third house of the legislature', a 'political' institution.

Judicial review The power of the Supreme Court to declare Acts of Congress, actions of the executive, or Acts or actions of state governments unconstitutional.

Now test yourself TESTED 

15 What is the power of judicial review?
16 How did it come about?
17 What does it mean to say that this power turns the Court into a 'quasi-legislative body'?

Answers on p. 116

Compare

There is no doubt that judicial review can have a significant effect on the actions of the executive. Can you think of three examples of judicial review in the UK that have had an important effect on the government of the day?

Judicial activism and judicial restraint

In a democracy, the people rule themselves through elected, accountable officials. But what if the courts — unelected and largely unaccountable — overturn the actions of these directly elected officials?

- Such behaviour by the courts is often referred to as judicial activism.
- If the courts tend to defer to the actions and decisions of elected officials — Congress and the president — this is referred to as judicial restraint.

Judicial activism

REVISED 

- An activist Court is one that sees itself as leading the way in the reform of US society.
- It sees itself as an equal partner with the legislative and executive branches in shaping society and acting as a safeguard of civil rights and liberties.
- It is not inclined to be deferential to Congress or to the president.
- It often uses its power of judicial review to strike down Acts or actions of elected officials.
- But the term can be used with overtones of disapproval by critics of such a court.
- In such cases, judicial activism may be labelled as 'legislating from the bench' by an 'imperial judiciary'.

Judicial activism An approach to judicial decision making that holds that judges should use their position to promote desirable social ends, even if that means overturning the decisions of elected officials.

Judicial restraint An approach to judicial decision making that holds that judges should defer to the legislative and executive branches, and to precedent established in previous Court decisions.

Imperial judiciary A term used by critics to describe an activist judiciary that allegedly exceeds its constitutional powers and attempts to overrule federal or state law rather than interpret the law. The term is used to criticise unelected judges having too much power.

Remember

When discussing particular decisions of the Court, do so from an academic and philosophical perspective, not from a personal perspective. The examiner does not want to know whether you personally are in favour of or opposed to, for example, a woman's right to abortion.

Examples of recent cases in which the Supreme Court has clearly taken the lead in shaping US society in terms of its rights and liberties are:

- *Roe* v *Wade* (1973) — guaranteed a woman's right to choose an abortion.
- *District of Columbia* v *Heller* (2008) — guaranteed individual gun ownership rights.
- *Obergefell* v *Hodges* (2015) — guaranteed rights to same-sex marriage.

Judicial activism could also be seen in the case of *Bush* v *Gore* (2000), which effectively awarded the presidency to George W. Bush after a disputed vote count in Florida.

Judicial restraint

REVISED 

- A restrained Court is one that is more inclined to accept the actions and decisions of elected officials.
- It sees Congress and the president — not itself — as the shapers of US society.
- Where possible, it tends to defer to the precedent laid down in previous Court decisions (*stare decisis*).
- A more accurate term may be 'judicial deference'.

Stare decisis A legal principle that judges should look to past precedents as a guide wherever possible (literally, 'let the decision stand').

Now test yourself TESTED

18 What is meant by judicial activism?

19 Give two recent examples of the Court's decisions reshaping US society.

20 What is meant by judicial restraint?

21 What does the term *stare decisis* mean?

Answers on pp. 116–17

The Supreme Court and the Bill of Rights

The Constitution's framers wanted to guarantee the fundamental rights and liberties of US citizens (see Chapter 1).

To do so, they added the Bill of Rights — the first ten amendments — to the Constitution.

First Amendment: freedom of religion

REVISED

Zelman v *Simmons-Harris* (2002): the Court upheld an Ohio state programme giving financial aid to parents, allowing them, if they so choose, to send their children to a religious or private school.

- *Significance*: acknowledged that state government money could be used to pay for children attending religious, private schools.

Town of Greece v *Galloway* (2014): the Court allowed legislative bodies (such as town councils) to begin their meetings with prayer.

- *Significance*: strengthened individuals' rights to practise their religion in public, even in state-constituted and state-funded bodies.

Burwell v *Hobby Lobby Stores Inc.* (2010): the Court overturned the requirement under the Affordable Care Act (2010) (otherwise known as Obamacare) that family-owned firms had to pay for health insurance coverage for contraception as this violated the religious beliefs of some Christian-run companies. The Court reaffirmed this right in *Little Sisters of the Poor* v *Pennsylvania* (2020).

- *Significance*: strengthened individual rights of Christian business executives to run their companies along lines that agreed with their religious beliefs.

Remember

Don't use overly dated examples, except maybe when they are really landmark decisions, like *Roe* v *Wade*. But even then, always give a more recent abortion rights decision as well to show that your knowledge is up to date.

Remember

In your exam answers, don't spend time telling the narrative of cases, except in the briefest outline. We don't need to know about the people involved in each case. Get to the significance of the case — explain what the case illustrates.

First Amendment: freedom of speech

REVISED

McConnell v *Federal Election Commission* (2004): upheld federal law (Bipartisan Campaign Reform Act) banning soft money in election campaigns, stating that this ban did not violate freedom of speech.

- *Significance*: limiting campaign finance is not incompatible with the freedom of speech provision of the Constitution.

Citizens United v *FEC* (2010): ruled that when it comes to rights of political speech, business corporations and labour unions have the same rights as individuals.

- *Significance*: opened the door to unlimited spending by corporations in election campaigns, mostly funnelled through political action committees (PACs).

McCutcheon v *FEC* (2014): struck down a 1970s limit on totals that wealthy individuals can contribute to candidates and PACs.

- *Significance*: reaffirmed giving of money to candidates and PACs as a fundamental right.

Second Amendment: gun control

REVISED

District of Columbia v *Heller* (2008): guaranteed individual gun ownership rights.

McDonald v *City of Chicago* (2010): extended the rights announced in Heller to state and local governments.

- *Significance*: never before had the courts ruled this interpretation of the Second Amendment.

Eighth Amendment: death penalty

REVISED

Roper v *Simmons* (2005): declared it to be unconstitutional to sentence anyone to death for a crime they committed when under the age of 18.

Glossip v *Gross* (2015): declared that lethal injection did not infringe the Eighth Amendment's ban on 'cruel and unusual punishments'.

- *Significance*: the Court was clearly seen as telling us what eighteenth-century words mean in the twenty-first-century USA.

Remember

You can use these decisions in your answers as examples of the Supreme Court:

- guaranteeing and guarding the rights and liberties granted in the Bill of Rights (e.g. freedom of speech, freedom from cruel punishments)
- interpreting words written in the eighteenth century and saying what they mean today (e.g. 'freedom of speech', 'freedom of religion', 'right to keep and bear arms', freedom from 'cruel and unusual punishments')
- becoming a political institution, in that it is making decisions on policy that are fought over in election campaigns (e.g. death penalty, gun control)
- giving itself a quasi-legislative function (as it were, rewriting or deleting parts of the Bipartisan Campaign Reform Act and the Affordable Care Act)

Now test yourself

TESTED 

22 Give two examples of recent Supreme Court decisions relating to freedom of religion and explain the significance of each.

23 Give two examples of recent Supreme Court decisions relating to freedom of speech and explain the significance of each.

24 What was the significance of recent Supreme Court decisions on gun control?

25 What was the significance of recent Supreme Court decisions on the death penalty?

Answers on p. 117

The Supreme Court and public policy

As well as interpreting the Bill of Rights, the Supreme Court decides cases affecting matters of public policy that are at the forefront of US political debate.

Public policy Action enacted by government to deal with issues or problems affecting the public at large (e.g. education policy).

Abortion

REVISED 

Roe v *Wade* (1973): ruled that the state law of Texas forbidding abortion was unconstitutional.

- *Significance*: guaranteed a woman's right to choose an abortion as a constitutionally protected right.

Gonzales v *Carhart* (2007): upheld the Partial Birth Abortion Act (2003), which banned late-term abortions.

- *Significance*: established that a woman's right to choose an abortion could be legally limited.

Whole Woman's Health v *Hellerstedt* (2016): struck down as unconstitutional two parts of a Texas state law concerning abortion provision.

- *Significance*: a woman's right to choose was held to have constitutionally defined limits.

June Medical Services v *Russo* (2020): struck down as unconstitutional a Louisiana state law significantly limiting abortion provision in the state.

- *Significance*: even after President Trump had appointed two conservative justices to the Court, pro-life groups remained disappointed in their aim to significantly limit abortion provision.

Conservative justices Justices with a narrow view of the Constitution. A term usually used to refer to strict Constructionists who try to interpret the Constitution in a literal rather than loose manner.

Marriage equality

REVISED

United States v *Windsor* (2013): declared the Defense of Marriage Act (1996) to be unconstitutional and that it is unconstitutional to treat same-sex married couples differently from other married couples in terms of federal benefits.

Obergefell v *Hodges* (2015): declared that state bans on same-sex marriage were unconstitutional.

- *Significance*: shows how the Court can reshape US society on a contemporary and contentious issue.

Remember

You can use these decisions in your answers as examples of the Supreme Court:

- guaranteeing and guarding the rights and liberties granted in the Constitution (e.g. rights of liberty and the equal protection of the laws — Fourteenth Amendment)
- interpreting what words written in 1868 (Fourteenth Amendment) mean in the modern-day USA
- becoming a political institution, in that it is making decisions on policy that are fought over in election campaigns (e.g. abortion and gay rights)
- giving itself a quasi-legislative function (declaring a 1996 law unconstitutional)

Compare

The UK Supreme Court, while not directly modelled on the US Supreme Court, has both similarities to and differences from the US version. Create a version of the table below with reference to the UK Supreme Court — is it a political institution?

Debate

Is the Supreme Court a political institution?

Yes	No
+ Members are appointed by a politician (the president). + Appointments are confirmed by politicians (the Senate). + It makes decisions on issues that feature in elections (e.g. abortion, gun control, marriage equality) and over which the two main parties disagree. + Some of its decisions have a quasi-legislative effect: it is as if a new law has been passed, and passing laws is what politicians do. + Some have described the Court as 'a third house of the legislature'.	+ Its members are judges, not politicians. + The Court is independent — not subject to political pressure. + Justices do not involve themselves in party politics, elections, campaigning or endorsing candidates. + There is no such thing as a Democratic justice or a Republican justice. + Members make decisions based on legal and constitutional argument, not political ideology.

Now test yourself

TESTED

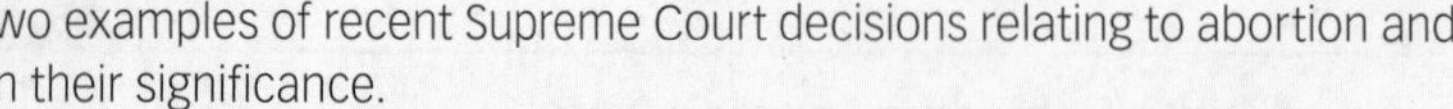

26 Give two examples of recent Supreme Court decisions relating to abortion and explain their significance.

27 Give two examples of recent Supreme Court decisions relating to marriage equality and explain their significance.

Answers on p. 117

The Supreme Court and federal government power

Through its power of judicial review, the Supreme Court also has the power to rule on the actions of both Congress and the president, and to decide when, in the Court's judgement, they exceed their constitutional powers.

National Federation of Independent Business v *Sebelius* (2012): upheld most of the provisions of the Affordable Care Act (2010) but ruled that the Act's requirement that every American had either to get health insurance or to pay a penalty could not be justified by Congress's powers under the Commerce Clause, only by its power to collect taxes.

National Labor Relations Board v *Noel Canning* (2014): declared President Obama's 'recess appointments' to the NLRB in 2012 to be unconstitutional as the Senate was not technically in recess.

Trump v *Vance* (2020): declared President Trump's claim of immunity from local law enforcement unconstitutional.

- *Significance*: the Court shows its power to say what Congress and the president can and cannot do according to its interpretation of their respective constitutional powers.

Remember

You can use these decisions in your answers as examples of the Supreme Court:

- interpreting the words of the Constitution, written centuries ago, and saying what they mean in the twenty-first-century USA
- acting as an umpire over the checks and balances of the Constitution
- preventing either branch of government from exceeding its powers

Now test yourself TESTED

28 Give an example of a recent Supreme Court decision on the powers of Congress.

29 Give an example of a recent Supreme Court decision on the powers of the president.

Answers on p. 117

Checks on the power of the Supreme Court

The Supreme Court, like the other two branches of the federal government, is subject to various checks and balances. These include the following.

Checks by Congress

REVISED

- The Senate has the power to confirm or reject appointments.
- Congress fixes the numerical size of the Court.
- Congress has the power of impeachment of individual judges — even the threat of impeachment is a check because it may act as a disincentive for a justice to completely overrule a decision or action carried out by the elected Congress.
- Congress can initiate constitutional amendments that would have the effect of overturning the Court's decision.

Checks by the president

REVISED

- The president has the power to nominate justices.
- Presidents can decide whether to throw their political weight behind a decision of the Court, thereby either enhancing or decreasing the Court's perceived legitimacy.

Other checks

REVISED

- The Court has no power of initiation: it must wait for cases to be brought before it.
- The Court has no enforcement powers: it is dependent on the other branches of government and/or the rule of law for implementation of and obedience to Court decisions.
- Public opinion: if the Court makes decisions that are regarded as wrong by a majority of the public, the Court loses some of its legitimacy.
- The Court is checked by itself — by decisions it has already made.
- The Court can overturn a previous decision of the Court: for example, the decision in *Ramos* v *Louisiana* (2020) overturned the Court's decision in *Apodaca* v *Oregon* (1972).
- The Court is checked by the Constitution — although certain parts of the Constitution are open to the Court's interpretation, other parts are very specific.

Remember

These checks would form a significant part of an answer to a question about whether the Supreme Court has 'too much power'.

Debate

Does the Supreme Court have too much power?

Yes	No
+ The Court gave itself the power of judicial review. + It has declared more Acts of Congress unconstitutional as the decades have passed. + It has made decisions that are out of line with the majority of public opinion. + It is an unelected body. + It is a largely unaccountable body. + Some critics would say it has abused its power to bring about significant policy change (e.g. abortion, same-sex marriage). + It could be seen in this way when justices believe in a living Constitution.	+ It is checked by Congress, which may initiate constitutional amendments, effectively overriding Court decisions. + Congress has the power of impeachment. + It has no initiative power: it must wait for cases to come before it. + It is dependent upon the rule of law and other branches of government to enforce its decisions. + Public opinion is a restraining force on the Court's power. + It is checked by the words of the Constitution where they are precise and not open to interpretation by the Court.

Now test yourself TESTED

30 Give two examples of the way Congress can check the Supreme Court.

31 Give two examples of the way the president can check the Supreme Court.

32 Give two other factors that can act as checks on the Supreme Court.

Answers on p. 117

Comparing the US and UK supreme courts

Origins

REVISED

The origins of the two supreme courts could hardly be more different.

The US Supreme Court:

- was created by the founding fathers in 1787
- was written into the Constitution (Article III)
- was the only federal court created at that time
- shared building space with Congress until 1935
- then moved to a purpose-built building on Capitol Hill

The UK Supreme Court:

- was created by Act of Parliament
- came into existence in October 2009
- was the most recent part of the UK court structure to be created
- replaced the Appellate Committee of the House of Lords as the nation's highest court
- was given converted building space (old Middlesex Guildhall) in Parliament Square

These differences reflect the structural and cultural differences between the USA and the UK:

- **Structural**: whereas the USA is based on a system of 'separated institutions, sharing powers' and checks and balances, the UK is based on a system of fused powers in which, until very recently, the three branches of government overlapped.
- **Cultural**: whereas the USA came into existence at one given moment — with the writing of the federal Constitution in 1787 — the UK has evolved gradually over centuries without a codified constitution.

Appointments, membership and tenure

REVISED

These structural and cultural differences also account for significant differences in the appointments, membership and tenure of the two supreme courts (see Table 4.4).

Table 4.4 US and UK supreme courts: structural and cultural differences

	US Supreme Court	UK Supreme Court
Method of judicial appointments	+ Nominated by the president + Require confirmation by the Senate	+ Nominated by the Judicial Appointments Commission + No confirmation required
Membership	+ Currently 9 members + Number fixed by Congress + Currently includes 3 women + Presided over by the Chief Justice of the United States + All justices hear all cases (unless recused)	+ Currently 12 members + Currently includes 2 women + Presided over by the President of the Supreme Court + Between 5 and 11 justices hear cases
Tenure	+ Life tenure + Subject to impeachment, trial and removal by Congress	+ Must retire at 70 if appointed to a judicial office after 1995; otherwise 75 + Subject to removal by the monarch following an address by both houses of Parliament

Revision activity

Using different-coloured pens, highlight the aspects of Table 4.4 which are examples of a) the rational approach, b) the cultural approach and c) the structural approach.

Powers and roles

REVISED

The most significant power of the US Supreme Court is its power of judicial review (see Table 4.5).

The UK Supreme Court also has the power of judicial review, but the terms do not mean the same thing in the two systems (see Table 4.6).

Table 4.5 Judicial review in the US and UK supreme courts

US Supreme Court	UK Supreme Court
✚ Not explicitly granted in the Constitution ✚ 'Found' by the Court in *Marbury* v *Madison* (1803), i.e. the Court gave itself the power ✚ Judicial review is the power to declare Acts (of the legislature) or actions (of the executive) of the federal or state governments unconstitutional ✚ Resulted in greatly enhanced political importance for the Court	✚ Judicial review does not allow the Court to declare Acts of Parliament unconstitutional because the Court operates in a system ruled by the doctrine of parliamentary sovereignty ✚ But it can declare actions of ministers to be ***ultra vires***, i.e. beyond the powers granted by Parliament ✚ This has given the Court increasing importance since its creation in 2009

Ultra vires Latin phrase (literally, 'beyond the powers') used to describe an action that is beyond one's legal power or authority.

Table 4.6 The powers and roles of the US and UK supreme courts

US Supreme Court	UK Supreme Court
✚ Final court of appeal for federal cases ✚ Also hears cases on appeal from state supreme courts ✚ Rules on the constitutionality of federal and state laws (judicial review) ✚ Rules on the constitutionality of actions of the federal and state executives (judicial review) ✚ Rules on the meaning of the Constitution ✚ Acts as interpreter and guardian of civil rights and liberties	✚ Final court of appeal for all UK civil cases and for criminal cases in England, Wales and Northern Ireland ✚ Cannot overrule or strike down the laws passed by the UK Parliament — though can interpret the laws passed by Parliament ✚ Rules on whether or not actions taken by ministers are *ultra vires*

Judicial independence

REVISED

Judicial independence is a vital ingredient in a democracy to ensure that judges are free from external pressures. Such pressure might come from:

- the executive
- the legislature
- interest groups
- the media
- other judges, especially senior judges

Judicial independence is protected in both countries by the fact that:

- judges have immunity from prosecution for any acts they carry out as judges
- they have immunity from lawsuits of defamation for what they say while hearing cases
- judges' salaries cannot be reduced

See Table 4.7.

Table 4.7 Judicial independence in the USA and the UK

In the USA	In the UK
✚ Judicial independence enhanced by life tenure ✚ Strengthened when justices decide a case in a way that is clearly not in line with the views of the president who appointed them (e.g. Clinton appointees who found against Clinton in *Clinton* v *Jones* (1997)) ✚ But seemingly undermined when judges appear to make politicised judgements (e.g. *Bush* v *Gore* (2000)) ✚ Under pressure when presidents make verbal attacks on the judiciary or on individual judges (e.g. Trump over the Court's decision on his travel ban (2017))	✚ Judicial independence was previously somewhat compromised when the Law Lords sat in the House of Lords (were part of the legislature) ✚ Still some ambiguities in roles of Lord Chancellor, Attorney General and Solicitor General ✚ Under pressure recently from attacks by politicians, notably about the High Court's ruling on the triggering of Article 50 in the Brexit implementation (2016) ✚ Recent media attacks on the judiciary as 'enemies of the people' after judges ruled that Brexit needed parliamentary consent (2016)

Now test yourself

TESTED

33 Give three ways in which the US and UK supreme courts differ in terms of their origins.
34 Give two reasons for these differences.
35 How do the appointment processes to the US and UK supreme courts differ?
36 How do the two supreme courts differ in terms of the tenure of the judges?
37 What does the term *ultra vires* mean? Why is it important in the UK Supreme Court?
38 Name three potential sources of pressure on judicial independence.
39 Give two ways in which judicial independence is protected.

Answers on p. 118

Using comparative approaches when comparing the US and UK supreme courts

REVISED

Table 4.8 shows how the three comparative approaches can be used when comparing different elements of the US and the UK supreme courts.

Table 4.8 Comparative approaches to comparing the US and UK supreme courts

Topic	Rational approach	Cultural approach	Structural approach
Origin of the Supreme Court		Created by the Constitution in the USA whereas in the UK the Supreme Court has been created only recently — making it easier to ensure complete independence of justices.	
Appointment of justices	The factors which influence a president's choice of nominee to the US Court — how do these differ from how a prime minister 'chooses' a new justice? The US president has significant ability to fill a vacant position with someone who suits their self-interest (e.g. their legacy).	The factors which influence a president's choice of nominee to the US Court — how do these differ from how a prime minister 'chooses' a new justice? The US president usually nominates a justice who shares their political opinions or at least has acted in ways which complement the president's political views and ideology (e.g. a Republican president is very likely to nominate a conservative justice).	A comparison of the structure of the process for appointing justices in each country.
Powers and roles			The differences in the powers and checks on these powers in each country due to the different political structures in the USA and the UK (e.g. parliamentary sovereignty; constitutional checks and balances; separation of powers; federalism versus unitary system). Comparing the power of judicial review in each country.
Judicial independence	How the concept of life tenure may influence judicial behaviour in both countries.	The pressure that judges come under from the media at times. Examples of when either supreme court has been forced to make political judgements (e.g. in the case of Brexit in the UK and the *Bush* v *Gore* election result in the USA in 2000).	The concept of the separation of powers in the USA as compared with the fusion of powers in the UK system.

Summary

You should now have an understanding of:

- the membership of the Supreme Court
- the philosophy of the justices
- the appointment and confirmation process
- the power of judicial review
- judicial activism and judicial restraint
- the Supreme Court and the Bill of Rights
- the Supreme Court and public policy
- the Supreme Court and federal government power
- checks on the Supreme Court
- the similarities and differences between the US and UK supreme courts

Exam practice

Section A (comparative)

1 Examine the differences between the US and UK supreme courts in terms of membership and tenure. [12]

2 Examine the role played by judicial review in the US and UK supreme courts. [12]

Section B (comparative)

In your answer you must consider the relevance of at least one comparative theory.

3 Analyse the differences in the origins of the US and UK supreme courts. [12]

4 Analyse the differences in the ways in which members of the US and UK supreme courts are appointed. [12]

Section C (USA)

In your answer you must consider the stated view and the alternative to this view in a balanced way.

5 Evaluate the extent to which the Supreme Court has quasi-legislative powers. [30]

6 Evaluate the extent to which the nomination and confirmation process of Supreme Court justices has been politicised. [30]

7 Evaluate the extent to which the Supreme Court could be accused of having too much power. [30]

Answers and quick quiz online

Exam skills

All Section B questions require you to 'consider the relevance of at least one comparative theory' (approach) in your answer.

This means that you need to make reference to at least one of rational, cultural or structural comparative approaches in your answer.

You do **not** need to focus your answer completely on one of the comparative approaches but you **must** make reference to at least one and display a knowledge and understanding of the approach.

The structural approach is the most commonly applicable approach to many topics but there will be instances when you will need to refer to the rational or cultural approach. The best way to make the choice is to work out whether the topic you are comparing in your answer involves individual political actors (rational), the ideas and culture of the society (cultural), or the actual structures and processes of the political system (structural).

Looking at question 4 above — *'Analyse the differences in the ways in which members of the US and UK supreme courts are appointed'* — there is a formal system for appointing Supreme Court justices in both the UK and the USA. This is a natural opportunity to refer to the structural comparative approach — by discussing the fact that the US Congress must approve all Supreme Court appointments whereas, in the UK, Parliament is not involved.

But you might also discuss the fact that a US president will choose a nominee who shares their political outlook, has similar opinions and is likely to make judgements that favour the president. This would require a rational approach because it involves an individual (the president) acting in a self-interested way (wanting to appoint someone who will make judgements in their favour).

However, you could just as usefully use the cultural approach — when discussing the fact that the appointment of a Supreme Court judge is for life and thus a conservative judge can still be making important constitutional judgements long after the Republican president who appointed them has left office. Hence presidents are able to have an effect on the political culture in the USA for a very long time.

Remember that you only have to refer to **one** comparative approach.

5 Civil rights and liberties

Protection of civil rights and liberties

Civil rights of racial minorities in the USA, and the pursuit of racial equality, have been advanced through various political means:

- Constitutional amendment to ensure and protect constitutional rights, e.g. the Twenty-Fourth Amendment (1964)
- Legislation, e.g. Voting Rights Act (1965)
- Decision of the Supreme Court, e.g. *Brown* v *Board of Education of Topeka* (1954)
- Presidential leadership, e.g. President Eisenhower's use of federal troops in Little Rock, Arkansas (1957)
- Citizen action, e.g. March for Jobs and Freedom (1963), Black Lives Matter protests (2020)
- Public policy, e.g. policing reform (although this has been criticised as not going far enough in the wake of the Black Lives Matter protests of 2020)

Remember

Don't turn your answers into an historical summary. Yes, you need to know the roots of the civil rights movement, but only — at the most — to refer to briefly, if relevant.

Civil rights of other societal groups relating to, for example, gender, disability and sexual orientation have also been advanced through a similar variety of political means:

- Constitutional amendment, e.g. Nineteenth Amendment (1920) — women's right to vote
- Legislation, e.g. Americans with Disabilities Act (1990) — rights of the physically disabled
- Decision of the Supreme Court, e.g. *Obergefell* v *Hodges* (2015) — right to same-sex marriage

Remember

Civil rights and liberties belong to groups other than those based on race. While much of the history of the USA's civil rights struggle is race-based, and indeed there are many recent race-based examples such as Black Lives Matter, always try to get an example of gender or LGBTQ+ or disability rights into your answer where you can.

Civil liberties in the USA (as seen in Chapter 4) have been mainly advanced and protected by the Bill of Rights (Amendments I–X of the Constitution) plus subsequent decisions of the Supreme Court.

Now test yourself TESTED 

1. Define the terms 'civil rights' and 'civil liberties'.
2. Name three means by which the civil rights of racial minorities have been advanced.
3. Give two examples of the ways in which the rights of other societal groups have been advanced.

Answers on p. 118

Remember

When giving examples in your answers, always use the most up-to-date examples that are relevant.

Civil rights Positive acts of government designed to protect people against arbitrary or discriminatory treatment by government or individuals.

Racial equality When people of all races and ethnic backgrounds have equal access to services, institutions, rights and freedoms.

Constitutional rights Those individual rights provided and protected by the US Constitution.

Civil liberties Those liberties, mostly spelt out in the Constitution, that guarantee the protection of people, expression and property from arbitrary interference by government.

Affirmative action

Affirmative action promotes equality of results rather than merely equality of opportunity (see Table 5.1). It was meant to lead to diversity and multiculturalism in education, employment, housing, etc.

In order to achieve this, quota programmes and busing (in school allocation) would be necessary.

Affirmative action A programme giving members of a previously disadvantaged minority group a head-start in, for example, higher education or employment.

Busing The mandated movement of school children between racially homogeneous neighbourhoods — white suburbs and black inner cities — to create racially mixed schools.

Quotas A programme by which a certain percentage (quota) of places in, for example, higher education or employment is reserved for people from previously disadvantaged minorities.

Table 5.1 Difference between equality of opportunity and equality of results

Equality of opportunity	Equality of results
+ Focuses on giving the same rights and opportunities to all + Focuses on the theory of rights and of equality rather than its outcome + Regards affirmative action programmes as 'reverse discrimination' + Believes all rights should be 'colour blind'	+ Focuses on outcomes + Focuses on giving advantages to previously disadvantaged groups in order to bring about equality in reality, not just in theory + Advocates such schemes as affirmative action and **quotas**

Affirmative action and the Supreme Court

REVISED

In various cases, the Supreme Court both advanced and regulated affirmative action programmes, especially as they related to school and university admission processes (see Table 5.2).

Table 5.2 Examples of Supreme Court decisions

Supreme Court decision	Ruled that...
Gratz v *Bollinger* (2003)	The University of Michigan's affirmative action-based admissions programme was unconstitutional because it was too 'mechanistic'; all minority students were automatically awarded bonus marks regardless of whether they had experienced disadvantage.
Grutter v *Bollinger* (2003)	The University of Michigan's Law School's admissions programme was upheld as constitutional because it used a more 'individualised' approach.
Parents Involved v *Seattle School District* (2007)	It is unconstitutional to assign students to public (i.e. state-run) schools solely for the purpose of achieving racial balance.
Fisher v *University of Texas* (2013)	The university's use of race in its admission policy must be subjected to a stricter scrutiny because it involved possible discrimination against white students.
Fisher v *University of Texas* (2016)	The university's admission programme based on affirmative action was constitutional. (A rehearing of the 2013 case)

Pros and cons of affirmative action

REVISED

+ Republicans and conservatives tend to argue against affirmative action programmes, claiming that they merely perpetuate decisions being made based on race.
+ Democrats and liberals tend to argue in favour of affirmative action programmes, claiming that they have made society more diverse and given equality of results to previously disadvantaged groups.

The advantages and disadvantages are summed up in Table 5.3.

Table 5.3 Affirmative action: advantages and disadvantages

Advantages of affirmative action	Disadvantages of affirmative action
+ Leads to greater levels of diversity + Rights previous wrongs — those previously disadvantaged are now advantaged + Opens up areas of education and employment that otherwise would be out of the reach of disadvantaged minorities + In education, creates a more diverse student body, thereby promoting integration and racial tolerance	+ Advantage for one group leads to disadvantage for other groups — 'reverse discrimination' + Can lead to minorities being admitted to higher education courses and jobs for which they are ill-equipped to cope + Can be condescending to minorities + Perpetuates a society based on colour and race

Now test yourself TESTED

4 What is affirmative action?
5 What is 'busing'?
6 What are 'quotas'?
7 Explain the difference between 'equality of opportunity' and 'equality of results'.
8 Give two examples of recent Supreme Court decisions regarding affirmative action.
9 Give three advantages and three disadvantages of affirmative action.

Answers on p. 118

Voting rights and minority representation

There have been significant strides in widening voting rights through:

+ legislation (e.g. Voting Rights Act (1965) and the re-authorisation of key parts of this Act in 2006)
+ voter registration drives among black and Hispanic communities
+ voter turnout drives among the same groups

But concerns still exist about:

+ the introduction by some states of a photo ID requirement at polling stations
+ the removal of voting rights following criminal convictions

Minority representation has increased steadily in recent decades:

+ **In Congress**: black members up from 16 in 1979–80 to 49 in 2017–18 and to 57 in 2020; Hispanic/Latino members up from 6 in 1979–80 to 38 in 2017–18 and to 51 in 2020. In 2021, 124 Congress members identified as black or Hispanic — making a record 23% proportion of congressional membership.
+ **In presidential candidates**: Barack Obama won the Democratic nomination and the presidency (2008); six minority ethnic candidates ran for the Democratic nomination in 2020 (e.g. Kamala Harris, Cory Booker). Kamala Harris became the first female, the first African-American and the first Asian-American vice-president in 2021.
+ **In the president's cabinet**: Barack Obama's initial cabinet (2009) was the most racially diverse to date — out of 15 heads of executive departments, seven were from minority ethnic groups; George W. Bush (2001–09) was served throughout by people of colour as secretary of state — Colin Powell followed by Condoleezza Rice. Donald Trump's initial cabinet (2017) included only three members from ethnic minorities, none of whom held any of the four top departments (State, Defense, Justice, Treasury). Joe Biden's first cabinet was announced in December 2020 and included ten women and eight minority ethnic Americans, from a total of 25 members.

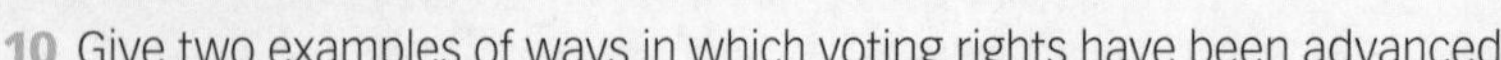

Now test yourself

TESTED

10 Give two examples of ways in which voting rights have been advanced.
11 Give an example of a concern about voting rights.
12 To what extent has minority representation increased in Congress since 1979–80?
13 Name two candidates from minority ethnic groups who ran for the Democratic presidential nomination in 2020.
14 How ethnically diverse was President Biden's first cabinet?

Answers on p. 118

Immigration reform

This issue has come very much to the fore during the past two decades.

It has been fuelled by concerns over illegal immigration, security fears following 9/11 and the fate of those Americans brought illegally to the USA by their parents in previous decades.

- George W. Bush tried to get immigration reform through Congress but failed.
- Barack Obama got Congress to pass the Development, Relief, and Education for Alien Minors (DREAM) Act.
- Obama also created the DACA programme (Deferred Action for Childhood Arrivals) in 2012, which gave some individuals who had entered the country as the children of illegal immigrants the temporary right to live, study and work in the USA.
- During the 2016 election, Donald Trump announced his intention to end the DACA programme, make the deportation of all illegal immigrants a top priority, and build a wall along the USA–Mexico border. By 2020 he had succeeded in closing the DACA programme and building a small section of the border wall.
- In January 2018, Trump's intention to carry through on his threat to end the DACA programme was a contributory factor in a short-term partial shutdown of parts of the federal government.

The impact of immigration reform on equality

REVISED

As Table 5.4 shows, immigration reform has had both positive and negative effects on equality in the USA.

Table 5.4 Immigration reform: positive and negative effects on equality

Positive effect on equality	Negative effect on equality
Development, Relief, and Education for Alien Minors (DREAM): stopped the deportation of undocumented immigrants who met certain criteria (e.g. they had been brought to the country as a minor).	DREAM was ended by President Trump.
Deferred Action for Childhood Arrivals (DACA): allowed 1.5 million people who had been brought into the country illegally as children to continue to live and work in the USA. This is very similar to the DREAM Act described above.	DACA was ended by President Trump.
Deferred Action for Parental Accountability (DAPA): designed to allow undocumented immigrants who had had children born in the USA to live and work in the country.	DAPA was overturned by President Trump.
	Framework for Immigration Reform and Border Security: introduced by President Trump, part of this policy separated illegal immigrant children from the rest of their family if they were arrested trying to cross the border. President Biden issued a series of executive orders to repeal this policy.

Now test yourself

TESTED

15 What did President Obama manage to achieve in terms of immigration reform?
16 What was the DACA programme?
17 What measures did President Trump propose regarding illegal immigrants? How successful was he?

Answers on p. 118

Remember

Always avoid expressing your personal preferences and prejudices in your answers.

Comparing the protection of rights in the USA and UK

The most significant difference is that in the USA, rights are entrenched in a codified constitution, whereas in the UK, with no codified constitution, rights are not entrenched and can be changed simply by Act of Parliament. This shows that different structures produce different outcomes.

So where do we find the rights of citizens in the USA and the UK? Consider Table 5.5.

Table 5.5 The rights of citizens in the USA and in the UK

In the USA	In the UK

+ Bill of Rights (Amendments I–X of the Constitution)
+ Later amendments, e.g. Fifteenth, Nineteenth, Twenty-Fourth, Twenty-Sixth
+ Laws passed by Congress, e.g.:
  + various Civil Rights Acts
  + Voting Rights Act (1965)
  + Americans with Disabilities Act (1990)
  + Fair Pay Act (2009)
+ Decisions of the Supreme Court, e.g.:
  + *Roe* v *Wade* (1973)
  + *Obergefell* v *Hodges* (2015)
	+ Acts of Parliament, e.g. Human Rights Act (1998), which incorporated the European Convention on Human Rights into British law
	+ Decisions of the courts that protect citizens against unlawful acts of government, e.g.:
	  + extent of government spying powers
	  + length of time police can keep DNA of acquitted persons
	  + whole-life sentences must be reviewable
	  + employers must respect religious beliefs of employees

Making links

The rights of US citizens are enshrined in the Constitution, especially in the first ten amendments. This is an excellent example of the importance of the Constitution to US politics and society.

Effectiveness of the protection of rights

REVISED

Effectiveness of the protection of rights is key to a liberal democracy. Constitutions and laws don't in themselves deliver rights.

+ Some see the protection of the rights of one group leading to a threat to the rights of another group: for example, same-sex marriage rights as opposed to the rights of groups and individuals that take an orthodox Christian view of marriage.
+ This issue has led to court battles in both the USA and the UK.
+ Effective protection of rights needs to be balanced against the need for security in the light of terrorist threats.
+ This is another issue that has led to much debate in both countries.
+ But a combination of legislative and judicial action means that the rights of racial minorities, women and those with physical disabilities are better protected than they were half a century ago.

Interest groups have played a significant role in both countries to promote the effective protection of a range of rights (e.g. ACLU, NAACP in the USA; Liberty and Stonewall in the UK). They have done this through various means:

- In the USA, interest groups try to bring influence on the legislature and the executive but most especially on the judiciary. There is much more focus on the judiciary in the USA than in the UK because of the power of judicial review.
- Interest groups may legally and financially support the bringing of potentially landmark cases to the Supreme Court for its ruling. For example, *Brown* v *Topeka* (1954) was effectively brought by the black civil rights interest group the National Association for the Advancement of Colored People (NAACP). In June 2020, a coalition of LGBTQ+ groups combined to file a lawsuit against the Trump administration, which had announced the rolling back of Obama-era transgender healthcare protections.
- They may also submit *amicus curiae* briefs to the courts.
- They also engage in building public support.
- In the UK, interest groups try to bring influence on Parliament, relevant government departments and (recently) the new Supreme Court. They also try to build public support.
- Interest group success in both countries will be determined by a number of variables such as financial backing, the balance of public opinion, strength of countervailing groups, access to the media, etc.

Revision activity

Construct a table comprising three well-known judgements passed by the US Supreme Court, and three of the rights mentioned in the Bill of Rights. For each of these judgements and rights, provide a short commentary on how they might not be upheld in practice.

Now test yourself TESTED 

18 What is the most significant difference between the protection of rights in the USA and their protection in the UK?

19 Name three places where the rights of US citizens can be found.

20 Name two places where the rights of UK citizens can be found.

21 Give an example of where protecting the rights of two opposing groups has led to clashes in the courts in both countries.

22 What issue regarding rights has the terrorist threat in both countries raised?

23 Name two interest groups from each country that are at the forefront of the protection of civil rights.

Answers on p. 118

Revision activity

Choose one of the US interest groups you identified in question 23. Research what issues and causes this group represents and what sorts of actions it has been involved in over recent years.

Using comparative approaches to compare the protection of rights in the USA and UK

REVISED

Table 5.6 shows how the three comparative approaches can be used when comparing the protection of rights in the USA and UK.

Table 5.6 Comparative approaches to comparing the protection of rights

Topic	Rational approach	Cultural approach	Structural approach
Bill of Rights (USA)		The US Constitution and the rights enshrined within it are central to US society and to an American's sense of identity.	The Bill of Rights consists of the first ten amendments to the US Constitution — a fundamental structure of the US political process.
Other constitutional amendments (USA)		The US Constitution and the rights enshrined within it are central to US society and to an American's sense of identity.	Civil rights are protected by the US Constitution — a fundamental structure of the US political process.
Laws made by Congress (USA)			Discussion of the legislative process in the USA.
Decisions of the Supreme Court (USA)			Discussion of the judicial process in the USA.
Acts of Parliament (UK)			Discussion of the legislative process in the UK.
Decisions made by the courts (UK)			Discussion of the judicial process in the UK.

Summary

You should now have an understanding of:

- civil rights and liberties
- affirmative action
- voting rights
- minority representation
- immigration reform
- the similarities and differences between the protection of rights in the USA and UK
- how to use different comparative approaches to compare civil rights and liberties in the USA and UK

Exam practice

Section A (comparative)

1 Examine the role interest groups play in the protection of rights in the USA and UK. [12]

Section B (comparative)

In your answer you must consider the relevance of at least one comparative theory.

2 Analyse the differences between the ways in which rights are protected in the USA and UK. [12]

Section C (USA)

In your answer you must consider the stated view and the alternative to this view in a balanced way.

3 Evaluate the extent to which decisions of the Supreme Court have weakened affirmative action programmes in the USA. [30]

4 Evaluate the extent to which voting rights and minority representation in the USA have improved since the 1960s. [30]

Answers and quick quiz online

Exam skills

All Section C questions ask you to evaluate (see Exam Skills on page 20) the **extent** to which something has happened. This means that you have to consider the size or scale of something. So in question 4 in Section C above, you need to evaluate **to what degree** voting rights and minority representation have improved since the 1960s. Have they increased significantly? What were they like in the 1960s? How have they changed now? Have they changed a lot or only a little? Are there still issues and concerns about voting rights and minority representation?

Presidential elections

Frequency and requirements

REVISED

When presidential elections occur

Fixed-term elections are held every four years (Article II).

If the president dies in office, resigns or is removed from office by impeachment, the vice president automatically and immediately becomes president and serves out the remainder of the president's term.

Federal law fixes Election Day as the Tuesday after the first Monday in November (i.e. between 2 and 8 November).

Requirements for a presidential candidate

Constitutional requirements for a presidential candidate are:

- natural-born US citizen
- at least 35 years old
- resided within the USA for at least 14 years
- also, since 1951, not to have already served two terms (Twenty-Second Amendment)

Other (extra-constitutional) requirements:

- political experience (though neither Eisenhower nor Trump had any)
- major-party endorsement
- ability to raise large sums of money
- effective organisation
- oratorical skills; telegenic
- sound and relevant policies

Now test yourself TESTED

1 How often do presidential elections occur?
2 What are the three original constitutional requirements to be president?
3 How does the Twenty-Second Amendment impact the requirements to be president?

Answers on p. 119

Stages in a presidential election

There are seven stages in a presidential election:

1. The invisible primary
2. Primaries and caucuses
3. Choosing vice presidential candidate(s)
4. National party conventions
5. General election campaign
6. Election Day
7. Electoral College voting

We will look at each of these in turn.

Invisible primary The period between candidates declaring an intention to run for the presidency and the first primaries and caucuses.

The invisible primary

REVISED

The invisible primary period — effectively the calendar year before the election — features:

- candidate announcements
- televised party debates
- fundraising
- higher national name recognition for lesser-known candidates
- opinion polls showing who are the front-runners
- endorsements by leading party figures (e.g. members of Congress, state governors, former presidents)

Debate

Is the invisible primary important?

Yes	No
+ The candidate leading in the polls at the end of the invisible primary is very often the one eventually chosen after the primaries.	+ It is possible to 'win' the invisible primary but go on to lose the nomination (e.g. Democrat Hillary Clinton in 2007–08).
+ Some candidates drop out during this period (e.g. 15 Democrats dropped out before the first state voted in 2020).	+ Candidates who drop out don't do so just because of the invisible primary but because they are ill-qualified and/or unpopular candidates.
+ They are critical for fundraising as the primaries and caucuses are packed into the early months of election year.	+ It does not test campaigning skills as well as the primaries do, and especially the caucuses.
+ First impressions in the televised party debates are important.	+ The focus is mainly on performance (in the debates and polls) rather than on policies.

Now test yourself

TESTED

4 What is the invisible primary?

5 When does it occur?

6 Name three important things that occur during this period.

Answers on p. 119

Primaries and caucuses

REVISED

This is the second stage of the presidential election.

- Primaries are held in mid- to large-population states (e.g. California, New York, North Carolina, Alabama).
- Caucuses are held in some small- to mid-population states, and especially in geographically large states with small populations (e.g. Iowa, Nevada, Wyoming).
- The use of caucuses declined significantly in 2020 due to the restrictions imposed in dealing with the Covid-19 pandemic.
- Any registered voter can participate.
- They have two main functions:
  - To show popularity for candidates among ordinary voters
  - To choose delegates to go to the national party conventions
- State parties decide whether to hold a primary or caucuses.

Remember

Notice the term 'caucuses' is plural — because in any given state that holds them there will be literally dozens of them all over the state. Hence we talk about 'the Iowa caucuses', not 'the Iowa caucus'.

Timing of primaries

- States decide on the timing of primaries and caucuses.
- The usual window is January/February to June of an election year.
- Some states schedule early contests (e.g. Iowa, New Hampshire).
- Some states deliberately coincide their contests on the same day as those of neighbouring states, creating a regional primary (e.g. Super Tuesday).
- Election cycles between 1984 and 2008 saw an increase in front loading, with more and more states pushing their dates earlier in the cycle. Although 2012 and 2016 saw some slippage in this trend, front loading was much in evidence again in 2020.

Types of primary

There are two different ways of classifying primaries. First, we can classify them by who is allowed to vote in them:

- **Open primaries**: in which any registered voter can vote in either party's primary
- **Closed primaries**: in which only registered Democrats can vote in the Democratic primary and only registered Republicans can vote in the Republican primary
- **Modified primaries**: like closed primaries, but also allow registered independents to vote in either party's primary

Second, we can classify primaries by how delegates are awarded in them:

- **Proportional primaries**: in which delegates are awarded to the candidates in proportion to the votes they get (there is normally a threshold a candidate must reach to win any delegates, usually set at 10% or 15%)
- **Winner-take-all primaries**: in which whoever gets the most votes in the primary wins all that state's delegates (allowed only in the Republican Party)

Early primaries and caucuses

Iowa traditionally holds the first presidential caucuses:

- They often attract very low turnout (just 2,108 voters in 2012 Republican caucuses).
- Turnout is also unrepresentative because Iowa is more than 90% white (74% in the USA as a whole) and caucuses also tend to attract the more ideological voters.
- Their record of predicting the eventual nominee is mixed (Senator Ted Cruz won the 2016 Republican caucuses, and Mayor Pete Buttigieg won the 2020 Democratic caucuses).
- But they can be crucial (e.g. Hillary Clinton's defeat by Barack Obama in the 2008 Democratic caucuses).

New Hampshire traditionally holds the first presidential primary:

- It often attracts a high turnout — 42% in 2020.
- It is possible to lose the New Hampshire primary but still win the party nomination (e.g. George W. Bush, Republicans, 2000; Joe Biden, Democrats, 2020).
- The most important thing for a candidate is to live up to or exceed expectations.
- Winning the New Hampshire primary brings a boost in opinion poll numbers, media coverage and money.

Primary A state-based election to choose a party's candidate for the presidency by showing support for candidates among ordinary voters. Primaries also select delegates to represent the state party at the national party conventions.

Caucuses A state-based series of meetings to choose a party's candidate for the presidency. They usually attract unrepresentative and low turnouts.

Super Tuesday A Tuesday in February or early March when a number of states coincide their presidential primaries and caucuses to try to gain influence.

Front loading The phenomenon by which states schedule their primaries or caucuses earlier in the nomination cycles in an attempt to increase their importance.

Remember

Don't forget that any registered voter can participate in the primaries and caucuses — they are not limited to party members.

Remember

Don't refer to proportional primaries as 'proportional representation'. That's something quite different.

Incumbent presidents and primaries

Incumbent presidents (e.g. Barack Obama in 2012; Donald Trump in 2020) have to compete in their party's primaries, but little or no attention is given to these primaries.

- Obama won 92% of the vote in the 2012 Democratic primaries. Trump won over 90% of the vote in the 2020 Republican primaries.
- But this all changes if the incumbent president faces a serious primary challenge (e.g. Jimmy Carter facing Senator Edward Kennedy in the 1980 Democratic primaries; George H.W. Bush facing Pat Buchanan in the 1992 Republican primaries).
- It was not coincidental that, although Carter and Bush won their primaries, they both went on to lose in the general election, having been politically damaged in the primaries.
- So the key for an incumbent president is to avoid a serious primary challenge.

Incumbent A person who currently holds an office — in this case, an elective office (the presidency).

Voter turnout in primaries

Voter turnout in primaries tends to be low — somewhere between 20 and 30% of eligible voters.

- Turnout varies from state to state (e.g. in 2020 it varied from 46% in the Montana primaries to just 9% in the Iowa caucuses).
- Turnout is higher in primaries than in caucuses.
- Factors that affect turnout in primaries and caucuses include:
  - Demography — turnout is higher among more educated, higher-income and elderly voters
  - Type of primary — open primaries tend to attract higher turnout as more people are eligible to vote in them
  - Competitiveness (or otherwise) of the nomination race — turnout is higher if the nomination race is competitive; lower if it's a one-horse race
  - Timing — primaries that are held after the nomination has effectively been decided attract lower turnout than those held when the race is still open
- Primary turnout was boosted in 2020 by widespread use of postal balloting due to the Covid-19 pandemic.

Debate

Are primaries important?

Yes	No
+ The presidential candidates emerge during them. + A large number of candidates are eliminated by them. + Delegates (who make the final decision about the candidate) are chosen by them. + They attract a large amount of media attention. + Lesser-known candidates see them as a way of boosting name recognition. + They test some presidential skills (e.g. oratorical, presentational, organisational). + They are much more important than they used to be before the McGovern–Fraser reforms (1970s).	+ Primaries often merely confirm decisions made during the 'invisible primary' (i.e. the candidates leading in the polls at the start of the primaries are often the ones eventually chosen). + What goes on in the media (e.g. televised candidate debates) is often more important. + Many presidential skills are not tested (e.g. ability to compromise, ability to work with Congress). + Many primaries choose so few delegates that they cannot be regarded as important.

Strengths and weaknesses

The strengths and weaknesses of primaries are outlined in Table 6.1.

Table 6.1 Strengths and weaknesses (advantages/disadvantages) of primaries

Strengths/advantages	Weaknesses/disadvantages
+ Increased levels of participation by voters + Increased choice of candidates + Process opened up to outside candidates (e.g. Obama, Trump) + A gruelling race for a gruelling job	+ Can lead to voter apathy + Voters are often unrepresentative + Process is too long, too expensive, too dominated by the media + Can develop into bitter personal battles + Lack of 'peer review' + Role of 'super-delegates' if the nomination is not decided on the first ballot (Democrats)

Remember

When presenting strengths/weaknesses, advantages/disadvantages, pros/cons in an essay, make sure that the second half of your essay doesn't just knock down what you said in the first half. Remember that what some regard as strengths, others see as weaknesses (a good phrase to use in such an answer). Also, one specific factor might be both a strength and a weakness depending on one's point of view.

How to improve the nomination process

There are various ways in which the nomination process could be improved:

+ Abolish the caucuses and replace them with primaries.
+ Do away with closed primaries, thereby increasing voter eligibility.
+ Rotate the order of primaries to increase geographic and demographic diversity.
+ Allow candidates to select their own delegates rather than having them allocated by the state party.
+ Institute four regional primaries, held on the first Tuesdays of March, April, May and June.
+ Hold a national primary.

Choosing vice presidential candidates

REVISED

The vice presidential candidate is chosen by the presidential candidate or by the incumbent president (when seeking re-election).

+ The nomination needs to be confirmed by a majority vote of delegates at the national party convention.
+ It used to be announced at the national party convention, but now is announced before that.
+ It is a big media event, especially when there is an element of surprise.
+ The announcement can give the presidential candidate a boost in the polls.
+ Candidates use different strategies for choosing their running-mate:
  + A **balanced ticket**, e.g. Biden–Harris (2020)
  + Potential for government, e.g. Bush–Cheney (2000), Trump–Pence (2016)
  + Party unity, e.g. Kerry–Edwards (2004)

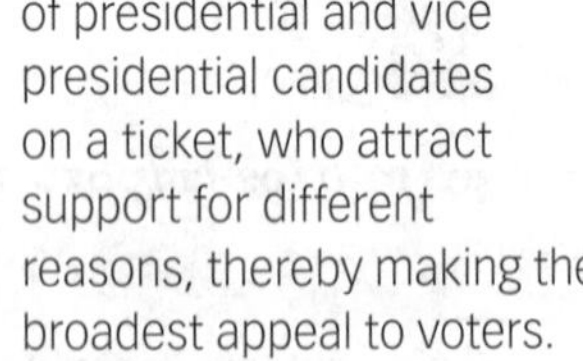

Balanced ticket A pairing of presidential and vice presidential candidates on a ticket, who attract support for different reasons, thereby making the broadest appeal to voters.

Now test yourself

TESTED

7 What is the difference between a primary and a caucus?
8 What are the two functions of primaries?
9 Explain the terms (a) Super Tuesday and (b) front loading.
10 What is the difference between an open and a closed primary?
11 What is the difference between a proportional and a winner-take-all primary?
12 How do primaries differ when an incumbent president is running for re-election?
13 What is turnout like in primaries and caucuses?
14 Give three reasons why primaries (a) are and (b) are not important.
15 Give (a) three strengths and (b) three weaknesses of primaries.

Answers on p. 119

National party conventions

REVISED

National party conventions are held by Democrats and Republicans as well as by some third parties.

- They are usually held during July or August.
- The challenging party (the one not controlling the White House) holds its convention first.
- A convention usually lasts for 3–4 days.
- It is held in a large city, usually in the East or Midwest (because of the time difference), e.g. 2016 — Republicans in Cleveland, Ohio; Democrats in Philadelphia, Pennsylvania.
- In 2020, the Republican Convention convened first in Charlotte, North Carolina, but then in Washington, DC, because of the Covid-19 pandemic. The Democratic Convention convened in Milwaukee, Wisconsin, but most of the business was conducted via the internet.
- The convention is attended by delegates, most of whom were chosen in the primaries and caucuses.
- Conventions have three formal functions:
  - Choosing the presidential candidate (but in effect merely confirming the decision made during the primaries)
  - Choosing the vice presidential candidate (but in effect merely confirming the choice announced earlier)
  - Deciding the party platform — that is, the policy document upon which the election will be fought (but in effect merely ratifying the document drawn up earlier by the party's platform committee)
- So it is the informal functions that are more significant:
  - Promoting party unity
  - Enthusing the party faithful (the attendees)
  - Enthusing ordinary voters (watching the key events on television or online)
- The key moment is the presidential candidate's acceptance speech, which is still covered by major TV networks.
- The candidate hopes for a post-convention 'bounce' in the polls as a result of the convention (but Trump's post-convention bounce in 2016 was just 1 percentage point).

National party convention The meeting held every four years by each of the two major parties to select presidential and vice presidential candidates and to agree the party platform.

Remember

Don't say that 'the conventions choose the presidential candidates' without explaining more carefully what you mean by that.

Debate

Are national party conventions still important?

Yes	No
+ The only time the national parties meet together. + Provide an opportunity to promote party unity after the primaries. + Provide an opportunity to enthuse the party faithful to go and campaign for the ticket. + Introduce the presidential candidates to the public. + Delivery of the acceptance speech. + Can lead to a significant 'bounce' in the polls. + Many voters don't tune in to the campaign until the conventions start. + A significant number of voters make their decision about whom to vote for at this stage.	+ Nowadays they make few (if any) significant decisions; merely confirm decisions made earlier that we already know about. + Television coverage has become much reduced. + Ordinary voters don't really see them as important. + Those held when the party is nominating the sitting president for re-election can be devoid of any real significance. + More balloons, hoopla and celebrities than serious policy debate and presentation.

Now test yourself TESTED

16 What are the three formal functions of national party conventions?

17 Give three informal functions of the conventions.

18 Give three reasons why the conventions (a) are and (b) are not important.

Answers on p. 119

The general election campaign

REVISED

This is when the inter-party contest begins.

- It began traditionally on Labor Day (first Monday in September) — though these days it begins straight after the conventions — and lasts until early November.
- It is a nine-week campaign.
- It is fought mainly in the media but with the candidates making campaign appearances in key states.
- Candidates can be hit by an unforeseen problem that damages their campaign late on — the 'October surprise' — which gives them little or no time to recover. For example, in 2016, FBI director Comey reopened an investigation into Hillary Clinton's use of a private email server while she was secretary of state. During 2020 Donald Trump had to deal with two problems — he was struck down with Covid-19 and so was out of the public eye for a while, and also was being investigated for allegedly paying only $750 in federal income tax in 2016.

October surprise An event occurring late in the presidential campaign to the disadvantage of one candidate, leaving them with little or no time to recover before Election Day.

Campaign finance The raising and spending of money to support a candidate or a political party in an election campaign.

Soft money Money donated to political parties instead of to candidates to avoid campaign finance limitations. Parties are allowed to spend the money on certain campaigning activities (e.g. voter registration and get-out-the-vote drives).

Political action committee (PAC) A political committee that raises limited amounts of money and spends these contributions for the express purpose of electing or defeating candidates.

Super PAC A political committee that makes independent expenditures, but does not make contributions to candidates.

Campaign finance

Candidates and parties need to raise significant quantities of money to campaign successfully. There are two main sets of legislation relating to campaign finance.

Federal Election Campaign Act (1974)

- This was a direct result of the Watergate scandal.
- It limited the contributions that individuals, unions and corporations could give.
- But loopholes were found.
- It saw the rise of 'soft money'.
- It was weakened by the Supreme Court decision in *Buckley* v *Valeo* (1976) and subsequent congressional legislation.
- It provided matching funds administered by the newly created Federal Election Commission (FEC).
- These funds dominated presidential campaigns between 1976 and 2004.
- In 2008, Obama opted out of matching funds, leaving him free from limits on money raising and spending.
- In 2012 and 2016, both candidates opted out of matching funds.

Bipartisan Campaign Reform Act (BICRA) (2002)

- This is often referred to as the McCain–Feingold Act, after its two initiators, Republican John McCain and Democrat Russell Feingold, both senators.
- The 2004 election saw the appearance of '527s', named after the section of the US tax code under which they operate.
- It led to the further widespread use of political action committees (PACs).
- The Supreme Court decision in *Citizens United* v *FEC* (2010) granted corporate and labour organisations the same rights of political free speech — and therefore political fundraising — as individuals and led to the setting up of expenditure-only committees, popularly known as Super PACs.

The main provisions of BICRA are as follows:

- National party committees are banned from raising or spending 'soft money'.
- Labour unions and corporations are forbidden from directly funding issue ads.
- Unions and corporations are forbidden from financing ads that mention a federal candidate within 60 days of a general election or 30 days of a primary.

Remember

Be careful when writing about the importance of money. It is somewhat misleading to say that someone 'needs a lot of money' to run for the presidency. You don't have to possess vast personal wealth to be successful. Neither Clinton (1992) nor Obama (2008) was particularly wealthy. Say, rather, that someone 'needs to raise a lot of money' to run successfully for the presidency.

- There was an increase in individual limits on contributions to individual candidates or candidate committees, also known as **hard money**.
- Contributions from foreign nationals are banned.
- It requires a 'stand by your ad' verbal endorsement by candidates on TV ads.

Hard money Money given directly to a candidate to assist in his or her election campaign.

Money raised by candidates, campaigns, PACs and Super PACs is spent on:

- organisation, manpower, and opening and running offices, mainly in swing states
- get-out-the-vote operations on Election Day
- campaigning, including travel and accommodation costs
- media, including buying time for political ads on TV and internet

Televised debates

Televised debates began in 1960, but then there were none until 1976. However, they have been held in each election since then.

- Nowadays there are usually three presidential debates and one vice presidential debate.
- The non-partisan Commission on Presidential Debates was set up in 1987 to sponsor and organise the debates.
- Only major-party candidates are invited to participate (except in 1980 and 1992 when third-party candidates — John Anderson and Ross Perot respectively — were invited).
- Different styles of debates have been used:
  - Candidates at podiums with either a panel of questioners or just one moderator
  - Town hall style with the audience asking some/all of the questions
  - Round table discussion with the candidates sat around a table with the moderator

Debate

Are the televised presidential debates important?

Yes	No
+ They can play a decisive role in the campaign (e.g. 1980, 2012). + They can affect the opinion polls. + They are especially important for the challenging candidate, who will be less well known. + A good sound bite from a candidate will be played repeatedly in the media in the days that follow. + A gaffe can seriously affect a candidate's chances of success (e.g. Gore in 2000).	+ In 2016, polls found that Clinton easily won all three debates, yet she lost the election. + Trump's numerous debate gaffes did not seriously affect his poll numbers. + Policy detail is rarely discussed. + They are not really 'debates', more the trotting out of rehearsed lines and catchphrases. + Viewership has tended to decline (though it was up in 2016).

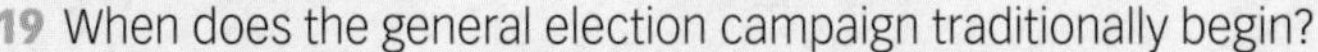

Now test yourself

TESTED

19 When does the general election campaign traditionally begin?

20 How long does the general election campaign last?

21 What is an 'October surprise'?

22 What is a political action committee (PAC)?

23 Give three main provisions of the Bipartisan Campaign Reform Act (2002).

24 Who now sponsors and organises the presidential debates?

25 Name three different styles of debate that have been used.

26 Give three reasons why these debates are important.

27 Give three reasons why these debates are not important.

Answers on p. 120

Election Day

REVISED

Election Day is fixed by federal law as the Tuesday after the first Monday in November (it falls between 2 and 8 November).

+ But more than 30 states permit early voting — it is estimated that some 47 million voted early in 2016. In 2020, largely because of the Covid-19 pandemic, there were 101 million postal votes.
+ Voter turnout peaked at 67% in 1960 and then dropped steadily to reach 51% in 1996.
+ Since 2000, voter turnout has varied before reaching a peak in 2020 as shown in Figure 6.1
+ It is usually difficult to defeat incumbent presidents seeking a second term (see Table 6.2).
+ Three of those who lost faced significant opposition in the primaries — Ford, for instance, was an unelected president; Bush had already served eight years as vice president as well as four years as president.

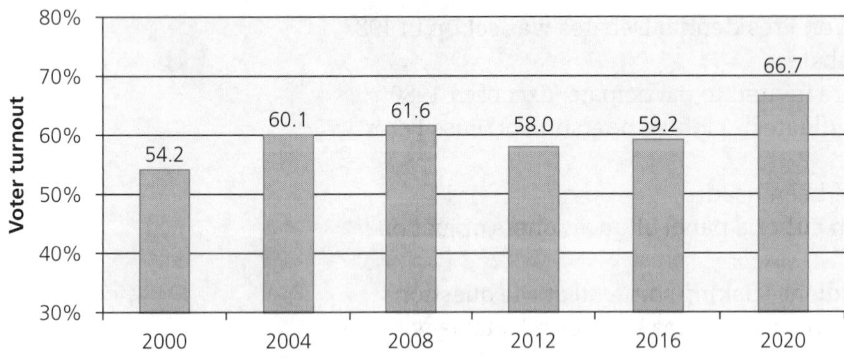

Figure 6.1 Voter turnout figures for presidential elections, 2000–20 (% of voter-eligible population)

Table 6.2 Presidents seeking re-election, 1964–2020

Year	President seeking re-election	Party	Result
1964	Lyndon Johnson	D	Won
1972	Richard Nixon	R	Won
1976	Gerald Ford	R	Lost
1980	Jimmy Carter	D	Lost
1984	Ronald Reagan	R	Won
1992	George H.W. Bush	R	Lost
1996	Bill Clinton	D	Won
2004	George W. Bush	R	Won
2012	Barack Obama	D	Won
2020	Donald Trump	R	Lost

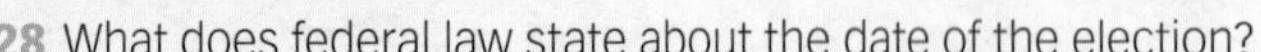

Now test yourself

TESTED

28 What does federal law state about the date of the election?
29 Approximately how many states allowed early voting in 2016?
30 What has happened to voter turnout in recent decades?
31 How many incumbent presidents have been defeated since the 1950s? Who were they?

Answers on p. 120

Electoral College voting

REVISED

How it works

- The president is not elected by the popular vote but through the Electoral College.
- Each state is awarded a certain number of Electoral College votes (ECVs).
- The number is equal to that state's representation in Congress — the number of senators (two) plus the number of representatives.
- Thus Wyoming has 3 ECVs (2 + 1); California has 55 (2 + 53).
- There are 538 ECVs altogether.
- A candidate needs an absolute majority (270) to win the presidency.
- The popular votes are counted in each state.
- The winner of the popular vote in a state wins all that state's ECVs — the so-called 'winner-take-all' rule.
- This 'rule' is not in the Constitution, only in state law.
- Two states — Maine and Nebraska — do not use the winner-take-all rule.
- The members of the Electoral College never meet together.
- They meet in their respective state capitals on the Monday after the second Wednesday in December to cast their ballots for president and vice president.
- In 2020, the Supreme Court declared that states could require Electors to vote for the state's popular vote winner, thereby eliminating the problem of 'faithless Electors'.
- They send their results to the vice president, who formally counts and announces the Electoral College votes in Congress in early January.
  - In January 2021 this normally straightforward event was marred by a violent protest by Trump supporters refusing to accept the election outcome. Subsequently they gained entry to Congress while the vote count was taking place. Politicians were forced to take cover but returned to the chamber later that evening to complete the count.
- If no candidate wins an overall majority:
  - The president is elected by the House of Representatives (one vote per state delegation), with 26 votes (out of 50) required to win.
  - The vice president is elected by the Senate, with 51 votes (out of 100) required to win.
- This has occurred only twice: in 1800 and 1824.

Electoral College The institution established by the Founding Fathers to elect the president and vice president indirectly. The Electors cast their ballots in their state capitals.

Remember

You must say an **absolute** majority, i.e. more than everyone else put together: 50% + 1.

Rogue/faithless Elector An Elector in the Electoral College who casts their ballot for a candidate other than the one who won the popular vote in their state.

Remember

You really do need to know how the Electoral College works. So learn it! Too many candidates just don't.

Strengths and weaknesses

The strengths and weaknesses of the Electoral College are outlined in Table 6.3.

Table 6.3 Strengths and weaknesses (advantages/disadvantages) of the Electoral College

Strengths/advantages	Weaknesses/disadvantages
+ It preserves the voice of the small-population states (Table 6.4). + It usually promotes a two-horse race, with the winner receiving more than 50% of the popular vote (Table 6.5).	+ Small-population states are over-represented. + The winner-take-all system can distort the result. + It is possible for the loser of the popular vote to win the Electoral College vote (Table 6.5). + It is unfair to national third parties (Table 6.6). + There is a potential problem if the Electoral College is deadlocked. + Faithless Electors have been able to cast their Electoral College votes against the will of the voters (Table 6.7), although this was curbed by the Supreme Court in 2020.

Table 6.4 Number of people per Electoral College vote: five smallest and five largest states (thousands)

State	Number of people per Electoral College vote (thousands)
Five smallest-population states	
Wyoming	195
Vermont	208
Alaska	247
North Dakota	253
South Dakota	288
Five largest-population states	
Illinois	640
New York	679
Florida	710
California	713
Texas	734

Table 6.5 Popular vote percentage of winning candidate, 2000–20 (popular vote winner in bold)

Year	Winning candidate	Winner's popular vote (%)	Loser's popular vote (%)
2000	George W. Bush (R)	47.9	**48.4**
2004	George W. Bush (R)	**50.7**	48.3
2008	Barack Obama (D)	**52.9**	45.7
2012	Barack Obama (D)	**51.1**	47.2
2016	Donald Trump (R)	46.1	**48.2**
2020	Joe Biden (D)	**51.3**	46.9

Table 6.6 Presidential election, 1992: popular vote and Electoral College vote compared

Candidate	Party	Popular vote (%)	Electoral College votes
Bill Clinton	D	43.0	370
George H.W. Bush	R	37.4	168
Ross Perot	Independent	18.9	0

Table 6.7 Faithless presidential Electors, 2016

State	To match the popular vote, Elector should have voted for:	Elector actually voted for:
Hawaii	Hillary Clinton	Bernie Sanders
Texas	Donald Trump Donald Trump	John Kasich Ron Paul
Washington	Hillary Clinton Hillary Clinton Hillary Clinton Hillary Clinton	Colin Powell Colin Powell Colin Powell Faith Spotted Eagle

Possible reforms

Direct election

Following 2000 and 2016 when the loser of the popular vote won the election, calls were made for the president to be elected by popular vote.

But this reform would have problems of its own:

- With a multiplicity of candidates, it was unlikely that the winner would gain 50% of the vote.
- There was a possible need, therefore, for a run-off election between the top two — further prolonging an already lengthy process.
- This could be brought about only by a constitutional amendment — which is highly unlikely.

Congressional district system

This system is currently used in Maine and Nebraska.

- One ECV is allocated to the winner in each congressional district.
- Two ECVs are allocated to the state-wide winner.
- In 2016, Maine split its ECVs — Clinton 3, Trump 1.

But this reform would also have problems of its own:

- In 2000, it would have made the result even less proportionate: Bush would have won 288 ECVs on the basis of 47.9% of the popular vote.
- In 2012, Romney would have come within 5 Electoral College votes of defeating President Obama despite having lost the popular vote to him by 5 million votes.

Proportional system

Each state would allocate ECVs in exact proportion to that state's popular vote.

- This would render the Electors unnecessary.
- It would be much fairer to national third parties.

But a proportional system also has problems:

- It would make it far more difficult for any one candidate to gain 50% of the vote.
- Therefore, there would be a need for a run-off election (see above).

National Popular Vote Interstate Compact

Before the 2020 election, 15 states plus the District of Columbia formed the National Popular Vote Interstate Compact (NPVIC). This is an agreement among these states to cast all their Electoral College votes to the winner of the national popular vote. But NPVIC comes into force only if it is joined by states controlling at least 270 Electoral College votes. These 15 states plus DC controlled only 196 electoral votes. Had NPVIC been operative in 2016, Hillary Clinton would have become president, having won the national popular vote by more than 2 percentage points.

Conclusion

For all its flaws, the current system seems likely to remain because:

- there is no widespread consensus on a better alternative
- it is highly unlikely that any significant reform would be legislatively or constitutionally achievable
- the suggested reforms also have significant problems

After the seven stages described above, and more than a calendar year of campaigning and voting, the president is sworn into office on 20 January of the following year.

Now test yourself TESTED

32 How are the Electoral College votes (ECVs) allocated among the 50 states?
33 How many ECVs does a candidate need to win the presidency?
34 How do most states allocate their ECVs?
35 Which are the states that don't? How do they do it?
36 What are 'rogue' or 'faithless' Electors? Give an example from 2016.
37 What are the two strengths of the Electoral College?
38 Give four of the weaknesses of the Electoral College.
39 Name three possible reforms that are suggested.
40 Explain what NPVIC is and what effect it could have on the presidential election.
41 Give two reasons why the current system is likely to remain in place.

Answers on p. 120

Congressional elections

See also Chapter 2.

When congressional elections occur

REVISED 

- House members are elected every two years.
- Senators are elected for six-year terms, with one-third being up for re-election every two years.
- So in each two-year cycle of congressional elections, all of the House and one-third of the Senate are up for re-election.
- The elections are held on the Tuesday after the first Monday in November.
- In years divisible by four (2016, 2020, 2024, etc.) they coincide with the presidential election.
- Elections in the years between presidential elections (2018, 2022, etc.) are called midterm elections as they fall midway through the president's four-year term of office.

Remember

To avoid confusion, use the term 'House members' to refer to members of the House of Representatives.

Midterm elections Elections for the whole of the House and one-third of the Senate that occur midway through a president's four-year term.

Locality rule A state law that requires House members to be resident in the congressional district they represent.

Requirements for a congressional candidate

Candidates for the House of Representatives:

- At least 25 years old
- A US citizen for at least seven years
- Resident of the state they represent
- Some states also include a locality rule

Candidates for the Senate:

- At least 30 years old
- A US citizen for at least nine years
- Resident of the state they represent

Nomination process

REVISED

Nomination is secured through congressional primaries.

- They are held between May and September of each election year.
- Winner of the primary becomes the party's House/Senate candidate.
- Incumbents rarely face a serious challenge.
- In a 38-year period (1982–2020), only 8 senators and 80 House members were defeated in primaries.

Trends in congressional elections

REVISED

It is possible to discern five important trends in congressional elections.

The power of incumbency is significant

- Between 2000 and 2020, House re-election rates ranged from 85% (2010) to 98% (2000).
- During the same period, Senate re-election rates ranged from 79% (2006) to 96% (2004).
- Most members of Congress leave by voluntary retirement or through seeking election to higher office rather than by electoral defeat.
- Reasons for high rates of re-election include:
  - incumbents' ability to provide federal funding for constituency/state projects
  - high levels of name recognition
  - fundraising advantages: incumbents can usually raise much more money than challengers

The coattails effect is limited

The coattails effect was last seen to be very strong in 1980 — Republican Ronald Reagan helped win 33 House seats and 12 Senate seats.

There was some coattails effect for Republican Donald Trump in the 2016 Senate races: three incumbent Republicans won seats they were expected to lose in states where Trump ran unexpectedly well.

Split-ticket voting is declining

The number of congressional districts that voted for a presidential candidate of one party and a House member from the other party (split-ticket voting) declined from 196 (1984) to 35 (2016) before falling again to just 15 in 2020.

The number of states voting for a presidential candidate of one party and a senator from the other party declined from 6 out of 34 (2004) to zero (2016).

There are fewer competitive House districts

A competitive district is one in which the winner won by less than 10 percentage points at the previous election.

- The number fell from 111 in 1992 to 31 in 2016, but then increased dramatically to 72 (D34, R38) in 2020.
- This is significant because:
  - it makes it much harder for party control of the House to change hands
  - members from safe districts are more likely to cast party-line votes than are those from competitive ones
  - it therefore increases levels of partisanship

The president's party tends to lose seats in midterm elections

In the six midterm elections in the period 1998–2018, the president's party lost an average of 23 House seats and around 3 in the Senate.

- In the House, this ranged from a gain of 5 seats (1998, 2002) to a loss of 63 (2010).
- In the Senate, this ranged from a gain of 2 seats (2002, 2018) to a loss of 9 (2014).
- The reasons include:
  - without the winning presidential candidate on the ticket, House members from the president's party do less well
  - voters see midterms as an opportunity to register disappointment/disapproval with the president

42 In each two-year election cycle, what proportions of the House and the Senate are up for re-election?

43 What are midterm elections?

44 How do the qualifications for the House differ from those for the Senate?

45 What is the locality rule?

46 Give two reasons for the high rates of re-election in Congress.

47 What is the coattails effect?

48 What is split-ticket voting?

49 Give two ways in which the decline in competitive House districts may be significant.

50 Give two reasons why the president's party tends to lose seats in Congress in the midterm elections.

Answers on pp. 120–21

Coattails effect When an extremely popular candidate at the top of the ticket (e.g. for president or governor) carries candidates for lower offices with them into office.

Split-ticket voting Voting for candidates of two or more parties for different offices at the same election (the opposite of straight-ticket voting).

Straight-ticket voting Voting for candidates of the same party for different offices at the same election.

Remember

It is easy to give the impression that partisanship is, in itself, a bad thing. But politicians sticking to what they believe and to what they promised in their campaigns is not necessarily bad. Indeed, some voters will want them to do just that!

Summary

You should now have an understanding of:

- requirements for presidential candidates
- the importance of incumbency
- campaign finance
- the main processes to elect a US president, including the invisible primary, presidential primaries and caucuses, and national party conventions
- the selection of vice presidential candidates
- the general election campaign
- the Electoral College
- congressional elections
- midterm elections

Exam practice

Note: The specification does not include a comparison between US and UK elections or electoral systems.

Section C (USA)

In your answer you must consider the stated view and the alternative to this view in a balanced way.

1 Evaluate the extent to which presidential primaries are important. [30]

2 Evaluate the extent to which the Electoral College is in need of reform. [30]

3 Evaluate the view that the congressional and presidential electoral processes do not do what was intended. [30]

Answers and quick quiz online

Exam skills

In all exam answers you will be expected to include **examples** in order to illustrate the point you are making. This is despite the fact that exam questions rarely explicitly request the use of examples. You need to get into the habit of giving an example every single time that you make a point or put forward an argument. It goes without saying that your examples should be as up to date as possible, but older examples may be more relevant depending on the topic.

Try to get away from the habit of always writing 'for example…' before introducing an example. While there is a place for such a gateway phrase, there are many others that can be used, such as 'as shown by…', 'as happened in…', 'such as…', or 'as was illustrated by…'.

7 Parties and interest groups

Party organisation

The US political party system is largely organised as a reflection of the federal structure of government.

Parties are largely decentralised — organised mainly at the state level.

Think of them as 50 state Democratic and 50 state Republican parties, plus a national committee for each party.

Party system How a political system focused through political parties is organised.

Developments since the 1970s

REVISED

Since the 1970s, a number of factors have led to strengthening of national party structures:

- New campaign finance laws resulted in money flowing to the national parties and the candidates themselves rather than being raised by the state or local parties.
- Television provided a medium through which candidates could appeal directly to voters, thereby cutting out state and local parties that had traditionally been the medium.
- Emergence of sophisticated opinion polls allowed candidates to 'hear' directly what voters were saying without actually meeting them.
- New technology allowed national parties to set up sophisticated fundraising and direct mailing operations — later also via social media.
- Parties became more ideologically cohesive.
- National parties played a larger role in recruitment and training of congressional candidates.

All this meant that party organisation became more top-down rather than bottom-up.

Current state of play

REVISED

Each party has a national committee with offices in Washington, DC. But members of national committees are representatives from the 50 state parties.

- The party is headed by a national chair — mostly rather anonymous bureaucrats who are seldom in the public eye.
- National party conventions are held in each presidential election year (every four years).
- There is also congressional party leadership with committees to oversee policy making and campaigning.
- State parties are headed by state party chairs and hold state party conventions.
- At grassroots level, there is congressional district, county, city, ward and precinct level organisation.

Remember

In the USA, the Republican Party is often referred to as 'the GOP' — short for 'the Grand Old Party'. It's a useful essay abbreviation.

Now test yourself

TESTED

1 What is the main reason that US political parties are decentralised?
2 What organisation do the Democrats and Republicans have at the national level?
3 Give three factors that have led to the strengthening of national party structures.
4 Who heads the national parties?
5 What organisation exists below the national level?

Answers on p.121

Party ideology

The names of the parties suggest that they are not ideologically exclusive. So ideological adjectives are often attached (e.g. 'conservative Republicans', 'liberal Democrats'). Bush (2000) ran as a 'compassionate conservative'.

The ideology is often linked to a geographic region (e.g. conservative South, liberal West Coast).

The Religious Right is a labelled faction of the Republican Party that has become more and more influential in recent decades. Also known as the Christian Right, it is a sub-group which is linked to religion — Christianity in particular.

Ideology A collectively held set of beliefs.

Religious Right A faction of the Republican Party which supports strongly conservative policies. They attempt to influence policy making and politics in general from a fundamentalist Christian point of view. They advocate, for example, pro-life policies, prayer in school and capital punishment.

Remember

Don't get the punctuation wrong in 'liberal Democrats' — liberal (lower case), Democrats (capital). Likewise, 'conservative Republicans'.

As a general rule of thumb:

- Democrats tend to be more progressive on social and moral issues, as well as on law and order; they tend to favour greater federal governmental intervention in the economy and on social and welfare issues such as education and healthcare.
- Republicans tend to focus more on individualism and limited government.

Remember

When using such material in your exam answers, always include a caveat that these are generalisations. Not all Democrats or Republicans support or oppose a certain policy.

Growth of ideological differences

REVISED

The two major parties used to be ideologically wide and all-embracing: 'broad churches' was a popular phrase.

When asked 'Do you think there are any important differences in what Republicans and Democrats stand for?'

- In 1972: 46% said 'yes'; 44% said 'no'.
- In 2012: 81% said 'yes'; 18% said 'no'.

When asked 'Is one party more conservative than the other?'

- In 1984: 53% said, 'yes, the Republicans'; 32% said 'no, both the same'.
- In 2012: 73% said 'yes, the Republicans'; 18% said 'no, both the same'.

The Democrats and ideology

REVISED

Generally speaking, Democrats:

- have a progressive attitude on social and moral issues, including crime
- support greater governmental intervention in the national economy
- support government provision of social welfare

But the two major parties are not ideological monoliths.

- Not all Democrats self-identify as liberals, especially in the South.
- Some call themselves 'moderate' or 'conservative' Democrats.
- Many saw the 2020 Democratic presidential primary contest between Joe Biden, Elizabeth Warren and Bernie Sanders in terms of ideology: Biden more moderate; Warren and Sanders more liberal.

The Republicans and ideology

Likewise, in the Republican Party, not all self-identify as conservatives, especially in the Northeast and the West.

In general, Republicans:

- have a conservative attitude on social and moral issues
- advocate more restricted governmental intervention in the national economy while protecting US trade and jobs
- have an acceptance of social welfare but a preference for personal responsibility

However, some will qualify their conservatism, for example:

- 'social conservatives' — conservative on social, moral and religious issues (e.g. abortion, same-sex marriage)
- 'fiscal conservatives' — want to reduce the national debt and the federal budget deficit, as well as reduce federal government taxation and spending (associated with the Tea Party movement)
- 'compassionate conservatives' — seek to use traditional conservative beliefs in order to improve the lives of those who feel abandoned and neglected by government and society

Remember

The Tea Party is not a party! It's best described as a movement.

In the 2016 presidential primaries, Donald Trump appeared as a post-ideological candidate as he did not represent a single coherent ideology. He was:

- neither a traditional conservative like Senator Ted Cruz of Texas
- nor a traditional moderate like the party's previous presidential nominee, Mitt Romney of Massachusetts

Remember

When talking of a president and their party's policies, you may be tempted to do so in a subjective fashion — either for or against. Always resist the temptation!

Between 2017 and 2020, Trump was able largely to reshape the Republican Party to reflect his own priorities and policy preferences. Even his more outlandish comments and actions received very little if any criticism from congressional Republicans or from Republican governors, with a few notable exceptions.

Now test yourself TESTED

6 Define the term 'ideology'.

7 What is the prevailing ideology of each of the two major parties?

8 What is the difference between 'social' and 'fiscal' conservatives within the Republican Party?

Answers on p. 121

Party policies

It is possible to discern some clear differences between the two major parties in terms of policies.

Not, of course, that all supporters of either party have the same view on key policies, but there are discernible trends of support and opposition on key policies in the parties, as shown in Table 7.1.

Table 7.1 Trends of support for (ticks) and opposition to (crosses) some key policies

Policy	Democrats	Republicans
Increased spending on social welfare programmes	✓	✗
Death penalty	✗	✓
Gun control	✓	✗
High levels of defence spending	✗	✓
Stricter environmental controls	✓	✗
Stricter controls on immigration	✗	✓
Universal healthcare	✓	✗
Black Lives Matter movement	✓	✗

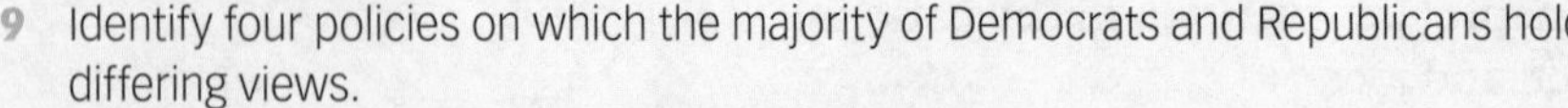

Now test yourself

TESTED

9 Identify four policies on which the majority of Democrats and Republicans hold differing views.

10 Which would you describe as the more 'progressive' party?

11 Which places more emphasis on 'limited government'?

Answers on p. 121

Coalitions of supporters

- US parties are best thought of as coalitions of interests.
- These coalitions are more narrowly drawn now than they were three or four decades ago.
- But both parties still need to put together a winning electoral coalition in order to win the presidency.

Gender

REVISED

In nine out of the eleven elections between 1964 and 2020, women were significantly more supportive of the Democratic candidate than men.

- Trump's 41% in 2016 among women voters was the party's lowest in a two-candidate race since Barry Goldwater's 38% back in 1964.
- In 2020 the gender gap for Trump was 11 points: he won the votes of 53% of men but of just 42% of women.

Gender gap The gap between the support given to a candidate by women and the support given to the same candidate by men.

The Republican Party's trend of poor showing among women voters is generally thought to be linked with policy differences between the two major parties, and more recently with Donald Trump.

The gender gap for the Democratic candidate in 2020 was 12 points, with Biden winning the votes of 57% of women and 45% of men.

The Democrats tend to take policy positions more favoured by women on:

- abortion rights (support)
- capital punishment (oppose)
- gun control (support)
- lower levels of defence spending (support)

Remember

The warning about over-generalisation is relevant throughout this section. Many women vote Republican, as do many Catholics and some Hispanics. Likewise, significant numbers of men vote Democrat, as do many older voters and those living in small towns.

Race

REVISED

The most significant minority groups in terms of the numbers who vote are black Americans and Hispanics/Latinos.

- Both give the majority of their votes to the Democrats — black Americans overwhelmingly so.
- Joe Biden won the support of 87% of black American voters in 2020.
- Hispanics are a growing group and therefore will continue to become an increasingly important voting group.
- Although they give a majority of their votes to Democratic candidates, George W. Bush won 43% among Hispanics in 2004, with 32% voting for Trump in 2020.

Class and education

REVISED

Class and education have become increasingly important determinants of voting, especially since 2016, because an increasingly disillusioned group of voters, distinguished by class and education, cast their votes for Donald Trump.

They were disillusioned because:

- they felt neglected by Washington politicians of both parties who had made promises to them during campaigns but had failed to deliver once elected
- of the effects of the 2008–09 economic crash — they believed that whereas the government bailed out banks and big business, they were left unemployed and unsupported
- they believed that their values, way of life and beliefs (e.g. in traditional marriage) had been swept aside and sneered at by a 'liberal elite'
- they felt that the USA in which they grew up — overwhelmingly white and nominally Christian — was fast disappearing

The group that most typifies these voters are white, older, blue-collar, non-college-educated voters who live predominantly in the Rust Belt states of the Northeast and the Midwest:

- White, non-college-educated voters made up over one third of the 2016 electorate and voted 66% for Trump — 71% among men in this group, 61% among women. They were attracted by Trump's 'Make America Great Again' slogan. These were the so-called 'Trump base' — his core, loyal supporters.
- Joe Biden increased the Democratic vote among white non-college educated males from 24% in 2016 to 34% in 2020.

Religion

REVISED

- Protestants, and especially white evangelicals, vote predominantly for Republicans (see Figure 7.1).
- Catholics traditionally support Democrats.
- Those who more regularly and frequently attend a church are more likely to vote Republican.
- Those who rarely or never attend are more likely to vote Democratic.

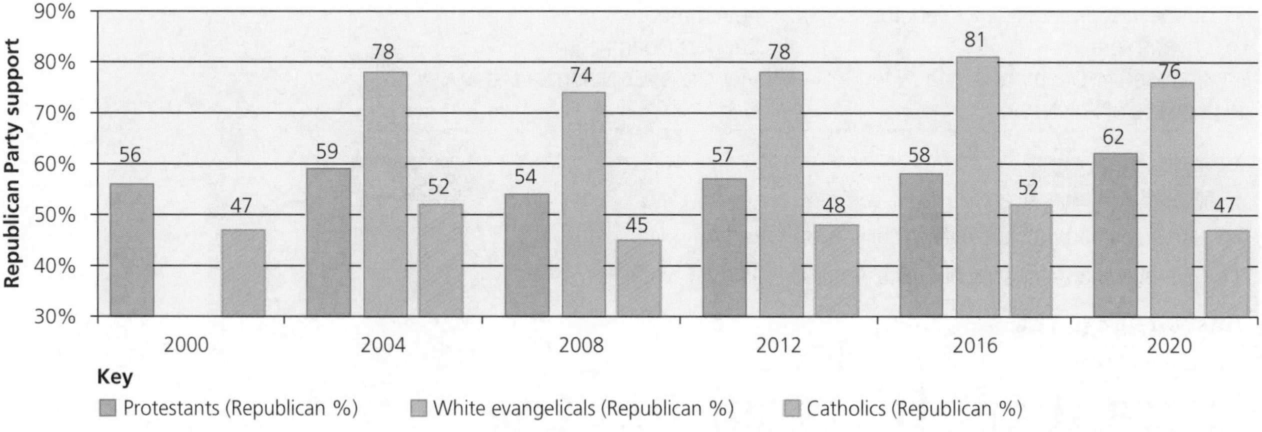

Figure 7.1 Republican Party support from selected religious groups, 2000–20

Other religious groups

REVISED

Both Jewish and Muslim voters make up a small share of the electorate but tend to favour the Democrats: 68% of Jewish voters and 64% of Muslim voters supported Joe Biden in 2020.

In the case of Muslim voters, this partly reflects traditional bias towards the Democrats, but may also have been a reaction to President Trump's comments and policies, such as a travel ban affecting seven Muslim majority states.

Now test yourself TESTED

12 Identify four groups that gave a majority of their votes to the Republicans in 2020.
13 Identify four groups that gave a majority of their votes to the Democrats in 2020.
14 Explain the term 'the gender gap'.
15 Give three reasons why Democrats traditionally win a majority of votes among women voters.
16 Give three reasons why older, white, blue-collar, non-college-educated voters felt disillusioned going into the 2016 election.
17 What was it about Donald Trump's campaign that appealed to these voters?
18 Name three 'swing states'.
19 What pointers are there in religion regarding party support?

Answers on p. 121

The polarisation of US politics

The 1990s brought a significant ideological shift in US politics.

- Both parties became more ideologically cohesive: the Democrats more liberal, the Republicans much more conservative.
- The nation became divided into what commentators called 'Blue America' and 'Red America' (see Table 7.2) — referring to the colours the TV networks use to colour maps on election night: blue for Democrats, red for Republicans.

Remember

When discussing polarisation and 'Blue America' and 'Red America', always make it clear that these are only trends and generalisations, but nonetheless they are useful indicators.

Table 7.2 Characteristics of 'Red America' and 'Blue America'

Red America	Blue America
+ Predominantly white + Overwhelmingly Protestant (and especially evangelical) + Rural, small town or suburban + Fiscally and socially conservative + Pro-guns + Pro-life + Pro-traditional marriage + Supporting limited role for federal government + Opposed to Obamacare + Viewers of Fox News	+ A racial rainbow of white, black, Asian, Hispanic/Latino + Urban + Socially liberal + Support gun control measures + Pro-choice + Pro-gay rights + Support an expansive role for federal government + Support Obamacare + Viewers of CNN and *Saturday Night Live*

Now test yourself TESTED

20 Give five characteristics of typical voters in 'Red America'.
21 Give five characteristics of typical voters in 'Blue America'.

Answers on p. 121

Current conflicts within the parties

The Democrats

REVISED

After eight years of Obama in the White House (2009–17), the Democrats were in a much weaker position than they had been when Obama was first elected.

- They lost the presidential election in 2016 — though their candidate won nearly 3 million more votes than her opponent.
- From 2008 to 2016 they lost 10 seats in the Senate and 61 in the House, losing control of both chambers.

- During the same period the number of Democrat governors fell from 29 to 16.
- They lost nearly 1,000 state legislative seats during the same eight-year period.
- At state level, the party in 2017 was at its lowest electoral level since 1925.

This led to conflict between the more left-of-centre, liberal Democrats — the Bernie Sanders wing — and the more centrist, establishment wing represented by Hillary Clinton and the party's congressional leadership team.

The election of Tom Perez as chair of the Democratic National Committee was seen by Sanders as a victory for the 'failed status quo approach'.

The victory of Joe Biden in the party's 2020 presidential nomination contest seemed to suggest that the party's moderate wing had prevailed. But we need to see how the party responds to the big issues raised in 2020 — the economic crisis caused by the Covid-19 pandemic and the Black Lives Matter protests following the killing of George Floyd.

The Republicans

REVISED

Meanwhile, a similar split had developed in the Republican Party.

- This initially showed itself in the appearance of the Tea Party movement and then developed into the so-called Freedom Caucus, made up of around 35 House Republicans led by Rep. Mark Meadows advocating a conservative and libertarian agenda.
- The Freedom Caucus members were influential in ending the speakership of Republican John Boehner in 2015 and have proved influential in a number of key House votes, most notably those concerning the repeal and replacement of the Affordable Care Act (Obamacare).
- There has also been a split in the party between what one might call the traditional Republican Party establishment and the supporters of Donald Trump, though the latter clearly won out during 2017–20.
- The establishment versus Trump debate shows itself in debates concerning such issues as free trade versus protectionism, the environment, immigration control, civil rights, racial equality, and internationalism versus 'America First' nationalism, as well as issues surrounding the 2020 election result.

Now test yourself

TESTED 

22 Give three pieces of evidence of the Democrats' electoral decline between 2009 and 2017.

23 Explain why this decline led to conflict within the party.

24 What splits have appeared within the Republican Party in the past decade?

Answers on pp. 121–22

The two-party system

A two-party system is a party system in which two major parties regularly win the vast majority of votes, capture nearly all of the seats in the legislature and alternately control the executive.

Evidence of a two-party system

REVISED

- **Popular vote**: in all of the last seven presidential elections, the two major parties have won more than 80% of the popular vote, on four occasions exceeding 95%.
- **Congressional seats**: after 2020, the two major parties controlled 533 of the 535 seats in Congress (senators Angus King and Bernie Sanders being the two exceptions, though both vote with the Democrats).

- **Executive branch control**: every president since 1853 has been a Democrat or a Republican.
- **State government**: by 2017, 49 of the 50 state governors were either Democrats or Republicans (Tim Walz of Minnesota is a member of the Minnesota Democratic-Farmer-Labor Party).

Reasons for a two-party system

REVISED

- **Electoral system**: the first-past-the-post electoral system makes life very difficult for national third parties.
- **Broad party ideologies**: there is very little room for other parties, except at the ideological fringes.
- **Primary elections**: these make the two major parties more responsive to the electorate, thereby minimising the need for protest voting.

Remember

A two-party system is not a system with only two parties!

Debate

Does the USA have a two-party system?

Yes	No
+ Democrats and Republicans dominate the popular vote in elections. + They also control nearly all seats in Congress. + They alternately control the White House. + They control state governments. + Leadership in Congress is organised and controlled by the two major parties.	+ The so-called two major parties are little more than coalitions of their respective 50 state parties — thus giving the USA a '50-party system'. + Some states are virtually one-party states (e.g. Massachusetts for the Democrats; Wyoming for the Republicans). + Third parties have played a significant role in some elections (e.g. 1992, 2000). + Many voters are self-described 'independents'.

Now test yourself

TESTED

25 Define a two-party system.

26 Give three pieces of evidence that suggest the USA has a two-party system.

27 Give three reasons why the USA has a two-party system.

Answers on p. 122

Third parties

Despite the domination of the two major parties, third parties do exist.

There are different types:

- National (e.g. Libertarian Party, Green Party)
- Regional (e.g. George Wallace's American Independent Party, 1968)
- State-based (e.g. New York Conservative Party)

Some are permanent (e.g. Green Party, Libertarian Party); others are temporary (e.g. Reform Party, 1996).

Some are issues-based (e.g. Green Party, Constitution Party — formerly the Taxpayers' Party); others are ideological (e.g. Socialist Party, Libertarian Party).

Impact of third parties

REVISED

Third parties might be thought to have little or no impact at all as they rarely win a significant number of votes.

Nevertheless, they can have a significant impact in that they can:

- influence the outcome even with a very small percentage of the votes (e.g. 2000)
- influence the policy agenda of the two major parties (e.g. the Green Party)

Third parties can have some impact within certain states (e.g. the Green Party won 9% of the vote in the 2010 midterms in South Carolina).

Now test yourself TESTED

28 Identify three different types of third parties, giving an example of each.

29 Give two ways in which third parties might be said to have a significant impact on politics in the USA.

30 Identify three difficulties that face third parties in the USA.

Answers on p. 122

Comparing US and UK parties

Party systems

REVISED

Theories of party systems tend to distinguish between three overlapping formats:

- Dominant-party systems: some US states (e.g. Wyoming, Massachusetts); some UK parliamentary constituencies — where one party almost always wins all elections
- Two-party systems (e.g. the US party system)
- Multiparty systems (e.g. the UK party system)

As both the USA and the UK have a first-past-the-post electoral system at the national level, how is it that their respective party systems are so different?

- The UK, too, used to have a two-party system: in the 1955 general election the two major parties won over 96% of the vote.
- By 2015 that had fallen to 67%.
- After the 1955 election, there were just four parties represented in the House of Commons; by 2015 there were 11.

The answer lies in the cultural and structural changes that have occurred in the UK over the past six decades:

- The rise of nationalism in Scotland, leading to devolution and calls for independence from the Scottish National Party (SNP)
- The rise of nationalism in Wales, leading to devolution and increased support for Plaid Cymru (Welsh Nationalists)
- 'The Troubles' in Northern Ireland, boosting support for nationalist parties in the province as well as splitting the Unionists away from the Conservative Party

No such cultural and structural changes occurred in the USA.

Campaign finance and party funding

REVISED

Campaign finance is often a bigger issue in the USA than it is in the UK because US elections are more focused on the individual, whereas in the UK elections are party focused and campaigns are financed by the central office of each party.

Controversies do occur in the UK, however, when it comes to party funding — with great media interest in who the rich donors to each party are.

In both systems, scandals over election and party funding have led to widespread concern. This in turn has led to changes in the law. But then parties, groups and individuals often find ways around the new legislation.

In the USA, there is the added question of whether the new law is constitutional, often leading to a ruling by the Supreme Court (e.g. *McConnell* v *Federal Election Commission* (2004); *Citizens United* v *Federal Election Commission* (2010) — see Chapter 4).

Both the USA and the UK have tried state funding as a way to solve campaign and party funding problems:

- USA: federal matching funds were introduced in the 1970s.
- UK: the introduction of Short Money in the 1970s.

But in neither country has significant state funding of political parties been adopted and this is where the debate is to be found.

Debate

Should state funding for political parties be introduced?

Yes	No
+ It would end parties' dependence on wealthy donors. + It would enable parties better to perform their democratic functions — organisation, representation, creating policy priorities. + It would fill the gap created by falling membership. + It would lead to greater transparency. + It would help equalise parties' financial resources. + It would make it easier to limit spending. + It would encourage greater public engagement if funding were linked to electoral turnout.	+ It would reinforce the financial advantage of major parties. + It would further increase the disconnect between parties and voters. + It would diminish belief in the principle that citizen participation is voluntary. + It would lead to objections from taxpayers, whose money would go to parties they don't support. + It would reinforce the parties' role, which many see as an anachronism in the digital age.

Issues surrounding party funding can be interpreted in line with the structural theoretical approach:

- Structures create relationships within institutions.
- Within parties, there is a relationship between the party establishment and the party members, donors and supporters.

Party funding can also be interpreted in line with the rational choice approach:

- Major-party hierarchies will mostly be happy with the status quo.
- Third/minor parties will seek change.
- Each favours the funding method that benefits its situation.
- So the US Green and Libertarian parties and the UK Liberal Democrats are more likely to favour state funding than are the major parties in both countries.

Internal party unity

REVISED

Internal party unity can often be an issue for broad-church parties such as the two major parties in both the USA and the UK.

It is usually less of an issue for one-issue, nationalist, ideological third parties such as the Green Party or the SNP.

Party factions can be constructive (providing new ideas and policies) or destructive (party in-fighting for control of party agenda and leadership).

Party factions A group or groups within a single political party that share views and interests that are different from the rest of the party.

Party factions therefore have different aims and functions, such as to:

- accentuate certain policies (e.g. income inequality, low taxes, moral issues)
- focus on a particular ideological aspect (e.g. conservative Democrats, hard left, libertarians)
- reflect geographic, ethnic, economic, generational, religious groups (e.g. southern Democrats, Christian Right, one-nation Conservatives)
- widen voter appeal (e.g. Tea Party, Momentum)
- extol the party 'greats' (e.g. Reaganites, Thatcherites, Bennites)
- challenge the party establishment (e.g. Freedom Caucus, New Labour, Tea Party, Corbynistas)

Party policy profiles

REVISED

Differences in the historical background of the major parties is key to the differences in their policy profiles.

- Unlike the Democratic Party in the USA, the British Labour Party came out of the trade union movement and has been closely linked with socialism.
- Unlike the Republican Party in the USA, the British Conservative Party grew out of a landed aristocracy and the established church.

Nevertheless, there are a number of broad policy agreements between the Republicans and the Conservatives. Both:

- dislike 'big government'
- favour low taxation
- talk of being strong on law and order
- stress high levels of defence spending
- talk more about equality of opportunity than equality of results

Similarly, there are a number of broad policy agreements between the Democrats and Labour. Both:

- put great stress on the rights of minorities — gender, racial, sexual orientation
- stress the rights of workers
- favour 'green' environmental policies
- want equality of opportunity, leading to equality of results
- favour high levels of government spending on health, welfare and education
- tend to favour higher levels of taxation on the most wealthy to fund services for the less well-off

But there are a number of policy areas where the Republicans stand significantly to the right of the UK Conservative Party. For example:

- abortion
- death penalty
- same-sex marriage
- renewable energy
- national healthcare
- role of central government in education

Now test yourself

TESTED

31 Why did legal changes regarding party funding come about in both the USA and the UK?

32 Give three arguments for and three arguments against state funding of political parties.

33 What changes occurred within UK politics that led the UK to move from a two-party to a multiparty system?

34 Give three reasons why factions appear within political parties.

35 Identify three policy areas in which the Republicans in the USA and the Conservatives in the UK basically agree.

36 Identify three policy areas in which the Democrats in the USA and the Labour Party in the UK basically agree.

37 Identify three policy areas in which the Republicans in the USA stand significantly to the right of the Conservatives in the UK.

Answers on p. 122

Using comparative approaches when comparing political parties in the USA and UK

Table 7.3 shows how the three comparative approaches can be used when comparing political parties in the USA and UK.

Table 7.3 Comparative approaches to comparing US and UK political parties

Topic	Rational approach	Cultural approach	Structural approach
The degree of internal unity within parties	US Representatives stand for re-election every two years. This means they must always have an eye on what their constituents 'back home' think of them — voting for things that benefit their state or district rather than following the party leader.	Geographically there are lots of differences within political parties — a southern Democrat, for example, sometimes has more in common with a Republican than a northern Democrat.	The whip system in the UK Parliament ensures a strong degree of internal unity within political parties. The USA has a much weaker whip system.
Debates around party funding and campaign finance	US election campaigns are more individually focused than UK campaigns. In the USA, campaign financing for an individual candidate tends to be the most common, while in the UK fundraising tends to be for the political party.	In the USA, there is a tradition of candidates receiving funding from big business and interest groups — therefore there is much more cultural acceptance of this practice than there is in the UK.	UK political parties choose their candidates, fund their election campaigns and provide a system of support for their campaigns that does not happen in the USA.

Types of US interest group

Interest groups are quite different from political parties.

- Political parties seek to win control of government; interest groups seek to influence those who have control of government.
- They vary considerably in size, wealth and influence.
- They operate at all levels of government — federal, state and local.
- They seek to influence all three branches of the federal and state governments — the legislature, the executive and the judiciary.
- There are numerous typologies of interest groups (so you can use others and not just the one given below).
- But one easy typology is to divide interest groups into sectional groups and causal groups.

Remember

Do be careful, therefore, not to give the Green Party as an example of an interest group. Greenpeace is an interest group. The Green Party is, of course, a political party.

Sectional groups

REVISED

These groups seek to represent their own section or group within society (see Table 7.4).

Table 7.4 Sectional groups

Type of sectional group	Examples
Business/trade groups	+ American Business Conference + National Association of Manufacturers + National Automobile Dealers Association + US Chamber of Commerce
Labour unions	+ United Auto Workers + Teamsters (truck drivers) + American Federation of Labor-Congress of Industrial Organizations (AFL-CIO)
Agricultural groups	+ American Farm Bureau Federation + National Farmers Union + Associated Milk Producers Incorporated
Societal groups	+ National Organization for Women (NOW) + National Association for the Advancement of Colored People (NAACP) + American Association of Retired Persons (AARP)
Professional groups	+ American Medical Association (AMA) + National Education Association (NEA) + American Bar Association (ABA) (lawyers)
Intergovernmental groups	+ National Governors' Conference + National Conference of State Legislatures

Professional groups Interest groups which represent certain occupational or professional sectors (e.g. doctors, lawyers, teachers).

Causal groups

REVISED

These groups campaign for a particular cause or issue (see Table 7.5).

Table 7.5 Causal groups

Type of causal group	Examples
Single-interest groups	✚ Black Lives Matter (BLM) ✚ National Rifle Association (NRA) ✚ Mothers Against Drunk Driving (MADD) ✚ National Abortion and Reproductive Rights League (NARAL) ✚ National Right to Life (NRL)
Ideological groups	✚ American Conservative Union ✚ People for the American Way ✚ American Civil Liberties Union (ACLU)
Policy groups	✚ Common Cause ✚ Friends of the Earth ✚ Sierra Club
Think-tanks	✚ Institute for Policy Studies ✚ Brookings Institution ✚ Heritage Foundation ✚ American Enterprise Institute

Single-interest groups Interest groups which represent a single interest (e.g. gun rights or pro-life issues).

Policy groups Interest groups which have a wide range of proposed policies that they hope government will implement (e.g. the Sierra Club is an environmental interest group which develops policy in a wide range of areas affecting the environment).

Now test yourself

TESTED

38 What are sectional groups?

39 Identify three different types of sectional interest group and give an example of each.

40 What are causal groups?

41 Identify three different types of causal interest group and give an example of each.

Answers on p. 122

Functions of interest groups

Interest groups can be said to perform five basic functions, although not all groups perform every function (see Table 7.6).

Table 7.6 Significance of interest groups

1 Representation	✚ An important link between the public and politicians ✚ For many Americans this will be the most effective channel of representation for their firmly held views and grievances ✚ More effective than going directly to their elected officials
2 Citizen participation	✚ Allows citizens to participate in decision making between elections
3 Public education	✚ Groups educate and inform public opinion ✚ Warn of possible dangers
4 Agenda building	✚ Attempt to influence legislators' agenda priorities ✚ May seek to bring together different groups to achieve a common interest
5 Programme monitoring	✚ Scrutinise and hold government to account in the implementation of policy

Methods used by interest groups

Interest groups use several methods in fulfilling their functions. These include those shown in Table 7.7.

Table 7.7 How interest groups fulfil their functions

1 Electioneering and endorsement	+ 1970s reforms limited the amount any interest group could give to a candidate in a federal election + This led to setting up of PACs and Super PACs (see Chapter 6) + Groups actively support or oppose presidential or congressional candidates on the basis of candidates' policy positions
2 Lobbying	+ Provide vital information to busy legislators and bureaucrats + Hence many groups maintain offices in Washington — 'the K Street corridor' + Many employ former White House staffers and those who have worked in Congress (either as members or as staff) + Groups produce voting cues for members of Congress + They also produce scorecards in which they rate members of Congress on key votes relating to their policy area
3 Organising grassroots activities	+ Social media or phone blitzes on Congress + Marches and demonstrations — often aimed at state and federal courthouses and legislatures + Civil disobedience (e.g. lying down in the road to stop traffic, or forcing entry to a government building)

Power of interest groups

Interest groups have had a significant impact in a number of policy areas, including:

- **Environmental protection** — groups such as the Sierra Club and the Wilderness Society have pushed for stricter laws for environmental protection and were at the forefront of opposition to the Trump administration's policy of scaling back on environmental protection.
- **Women's rights** — such groups as the League of Women Voters and the National Organization for Women pushed unsuccessfully for passage of the Equal Rights Amendment to the Constitution in the 1970s and 1980s; they are now campaigning on issues such as equal pay and sexual harassment in the workplace.
- **Abortion rights** — both pro-life and pro-choice lobbies have been active for the past 40–50 years; they try to be influential not only in the abortion debate but in nomination and confirmation of judicial appointments, especially to the Supreme Court.
- **Gun control** — the National Rifle Association is one of the most powerful groups. It seeks to protect Second Amendment rights and opposes tougher gun control legislation. It has found itself more on the defensive following the deaths of 17 people in a Florida high school shooting in February 2018.
- **Racial equality** — the Black Lives Matter movement came to the fore following the killing of George Floyd in police custody in May 2020. BLM demonstrations occurred in cities and towns throughout the country. These were mostly peaceful but some attracted a violent and destructive element. The demonstrations gave impetus to both the prioritising of police reform and the removal of symbols of slavery. These debates dominated the 2020 elections.

Remember

It is easy in writing an answer to give the impression that just because an interest group exists and does something, it is therefore effective and successful. Try to be more subtle in your analysis. State what a group is aiming to achieve, then you can judge whether it is effective or successful.

Remember

Beware of mixing up 'pro-choice' and 'pro-life'. Pro-choice groups favour a woman's right to choose whether to have an abortion; pro-life groups support the right to life of the unborn child and are therefore against abortion.

Now test yourself TESTED

42 Identify three functions of interest groups.

43 Identify three methods used by interest groups.

44 Name three policy areas in which interest groups have been especially influential.

Answers on p. 123

Remember

Ensure that you have a wide range of examples of interest groups — not just the NRA.

Impact of interest groups on government

Impact on Congress

REVISED

Interest groups make an impact by using the following tactics:

- Directly lobbying members of Congress; attempting to influence legislation and the way members cast their votes
- Lobbying congressional committees, especially those who chair or are ranking minority members on relevant committees (see Chapter 2)
- Organising constituents — by phone, the internet and social media
- Publicising members' voting records and endorsing or opposing candidates

Impact on the executive

REVISED

They seek to:

- maintain strong ties with relevant executive departments, agencies and bureaus
- influence the drawing up and enactment of policy within their area of interest

Impact on the judiciary

Interest groups:

- take a lively interest in the nomination and confirmation of judges to the federal courts, especially those to the Supreme Court
- try to influence court hearings through *amicus curiae* (friend of the court) briefings, thereby presenting their views to the court in writing before oral arguments are heard

The American Bar Association (ABA) evaluates the professional qualifications of federal court nominees.

One of the most influential groups is the American Civil Liberties Union (ACLU), which has helped bring high-profile cases to the courts over such issues as protecting affirmative action and, more recently, transgender rights.

Debate

Do we need interest groups?

Yes	No
+ They provide legislators and bureaucrats with useful information and act as a sounding board in policy formulation. + They bring some priority order to the policy debate. + They broaden the opportunities for participation in democracy. + They can increase levels of accountability for both Congress and the executive. + They increase opportunities for representation between elections. + They enhance freedom of speech and freedom of association.	+ The **revolving-door syndrome** allows former members of Congress or of the executive unfair influence to lobby the institution of which they were once a member. + The **iron-triangle syndrome** perpetuates a cosy relationship between interest groups, the relevant congressional committee(s) and the relevant department or agency. + Inequality of groups — in terms of access, money, size. + They tend to favour the special interest over the public interest. + Allegations of 'buying influence'. + Use of direct action that breaks the law, including violence.

Revolving-door syndrome The practice by which former members of Congress (or the executive) take up well-paid jobs with Washington-based lobbying firms, using their expertise and contacts to lobby their previous institution.

Iron-triangle syndrome A strong relationship between interest groups, the relevant congressional committees and the relevant government department, which attempts to achieve mutually beneficial policy outcomes.

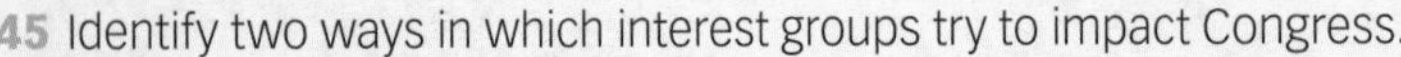

Now test yourself

TESTED

45 Identify two ways in which interest groups try to impact Congress.
46 Identify two ways in which interest groups try to impact the executive branch.
47 Identify two ways in which interest groups try to impact the judiciary.
48 Define the term 'revolving-door syndrome'.
49 Define the term 'iron-triangle syndrome'.

Answers on p. 123

Comparing US and UK interest groups

Electioneering and endorsing

There are far more elective posts in the USA than in the UK.

+ Presidential, Senate (second chamber) and state elections are all unknown in the UK.
+ There is also the possibility of primaries in the USA.
+ All this means that for structural reasons, US interest groups have far more opportunities for influence than do their UK counterparts.
+ But in the UK, there is a historically close link between organised labour and one of the two major parties (Labour).
+ It is true that trade union membership has fallen in recent decades, but the TUC is much more electorally influential in elections in the UK than is the AFL-CIO in the USA.

Remember

Interest groups can also be referred to as pressure groups.

Lobbying

REVISED

In terms of lobbying, because of important structural differences, there are far more opportunities for interest group activity in the USA than in the UK, in all three branches.

Legislature

+ The UK Parliament is more controlled and party disciplined than the US Congress.
+ The UK Parliament is largely controlled by the executive.
+ Therefore, with parties holding more sway at Westminster, interest groups tend to enjoy less influence.
+ But the House of Lords still offers interest groups opportunities as peers are not subject to party whipping to the same extent as their Commons counterparts.

Executive

+ Policy-specific interest groups will focus on appropriate executive departments — especially in the UK where the legislature provides fewer opportunities for interest groups.
+ In the USA, interest groups tend to focus more on congressional committees and rather less on executive departments and agencies.
+ Again, the difference is largely caused by the structural differences of separation of powers.

Judiciary

- There are significant differences in the political importance of the respective judiciaries.
- Hence lobbying of the courts is much more established in the USA than in the UK because the US courts have the power to interpret a written constitution and can declare laws and actions to be unconstitutional, and thereby null and void (see Chapter 4).
- US interest groups have a long and distinguished history of lobbying the Supreme Court and of being a major player in some landmark decisions concerning, for example:
  - equal rights for racial minorities
  - abortion
  - religious freedoms
  - freedom of speech
- But in the UK, where even the new Supreme Court must operate within a constitutional structure dominated by parliamentary supremacy, and there is no a codified constitution with entrenched rights, there is also no tradition of lobbying the courts.

Grassroots activity

Groups in both the USA and the UK organise **grassroots activity**:

- In the UK, where parties are more centralised and disciplined, this often means trying to influence one of the two major parties.
- In the USA, where parties are less highly centralised, influence is more likely to be aimed at the branches of the federal and state governments.
- In both countries, interest groups will seek influence through both mass and social media.

Grassroots activity Collective action at the local level.

What determines success?

REVISED

In both systems, interest group success will be determined largely by factors such as:

- size of membership
- amount of money available
- the group's strategic position in the political system
- the balance of public opinion
- strength or weakness of countervailing group(s)
- attitude of the administration (USA)/government (UK)
- ability to access the media

Now test yourself

50 Why are there more opportunities for interest groups to influence elections in the USA than in the UK?

51 Why are there more opportunities for interest groups to influence the legislature in the USA than in the UK?

52 Why do interest groups in the UK focus more on the executive branch than on the legislature?

53 Why are there more opportunities for interest groups to influence the judiciary in the USA than in the UK?

54 Identify four factors that help determine interest group success.

Answers on p. 123

Summary

You should now have an understanding of:

- party organisation
- party ideology
- party policies
- coalitions of supporters
- the polarisation of US politics
- the two-party system
- third parties
- current conflicts within the parties
- campaign finance in the USA and the UK
- the similarities and differences between political parties in the USA and the UK
- how to use different comparative approaches to compare political parties in the USA and UK
- types of interest group
- functions of interest groups
- methods used by interest groups
- the power and impact of interest groups
- arguments for and against interest groups
- the similarities and differences between interest groups in the USA and UK

Exam practice

Section A (comparative)

1 Examine the ways in which the importance of third parties in the USA and UK differs. [12]

2 Examine the factors that enhance the power of interest groups in elections in both the USA and UK. [12]

3 Examine the aspects that create a two-party dominance in the USA and UK. [12]

Section B (comparative)

In your answer you must consider the relevance of at least one comparative theory.

4 Analyse the differences in party systems in the USA and UK. [12]

5 Analyse the differences in the opportunities for interest groups to influence the judiciary in the USA and UK. [12]

Section C (USA)

In your answer you must consider the stated view and the alternative to this view in a balanced way.

6 Evaluate the extent to which third parties in the USA always lose. [30]

7 Evaluate the extent to which interest groups are a necessary evil in the US political system. [30]

Answers and quick quiz online

Exam skills

'By failing to prepare, you are preparing to fail,' said Benjamin Franklin — a sentiment echoed by a famous (and very successful) Premier League football manager some 200 years later! Whether you are a politician or a football manager or a student taking A-level Politics, the message is the same: you have to prepare in order to succeed. Of course, you need to prepare by fully revising everything before the exam and you can also prepare by testing yourself with past exam questions; but once in the exam room you need to continue to prepare — you need to **plan** your answers and **manage** your time effectively to put yourself in the very best position to succeed.

Practise this planning before the exam so that it becomes a habit.

Now test yourself answers

Chapter 1

1 The large-population states wanted proportional representation and the small-population states wanted equal representation.

2 A federal form of government; two houses of Congress — one with equal representation for all the states, the other with representation proportional to each state's population; an indirectly elected president.

3 Codified; a blend of vagueness and specificity; entrenched provisions.

4 A constitution that consists of a full and authoritative set of rules written down in a single document.

5 The legislature, the executive and the judiciary.

6 One of: the 'common defence and general welfare clause'; the 'necessary and proper clause'.

7 Enumerated powers are specifically granted by the Constitution; implied powers are merely inferred by the Constitution.

8 Reserved powers are those reserved to the states and to the people; concurrent powers are granted to both the federal and state governments.

9 Powers safeguarded by making them difficult to amend or abolish.

10 Either by two-thirds majorities in both houses of Congress, or by the legislatures in two-thirds of the states calling for a national constitutional convention.

11 Either by three-quarters of the state legislatures, or by ratifying conventions in three-quarters of the states.

12 Advantages — three of:
- Super-majorities ensure against a small majority being able to impose its will on the majority.
- The lengthy and complicated process makes it less likely that the Constitution will be amended on a merely temporary issue.
- It ensures that both the federal and state governments must favour a proposal.
- It gives a magnified voice to the smaller-population states (through Senate's role and the requirement for agreement of three-quarters of state legislatures).
- Provision for a constitutional convention called by the states ensures against a veto being operated by Congress on the initiation of amendments.

Disadvantages — three of:
- It makes it overly difficult for the Constitution to be amended, thereby perpetuating what some see as outdated provisions, e.g. the Electoral College.
- It makes possible the thwarting of the will of the majority by a small and possibly unrepresentative minority.
- The lengthy and complicated process nonetheless allowed the Prohibition amendment to be passed (1918).
- The difficulty of formal amendment enhances power of the (unelected) Supreme Court to make interpretative amendments.
- The voice of small-population states is overly represented.

13 The Bill of Rights.

14 Two of:
- Slavery prohibited (Thirteenth Amendment, 1865)
- Federal government granted power to impose income tax (Sixteenth Amendment, 1913)
- Direct election of the Senate (Seventeenth Amendment, 1913)
- Two-term limit for the president (Twenty-Second Amendment, 1951)
- Presidential succession and disability procedures (Twenty-Fifth Amendment, 1967)
- Voting age lowered to 18 (Twenty-Sixth Amendment, 1971)

15 Two of:
- The Founding Fathers created a deliberately difficult process.
- The Constitution is, in parts, deliberately vague and has therefore evolved without the need for formal amendment.
- The Supreme Court has the power of judicial review (see Chapter 4).
- Americans have become cautious about tampering with the Constitution.

16 Separation of powers, checks and balances, federalism, bipartisanship, limited government.

17 A theory of government whereby political power is distributed among the legislature, the executive and the judiciary, each acting both independently and interdependently.

18 Institutions; powers.

19

President on Congress	Veto a bill
President on federal courts	Nominate judges Pardon
Congress on the president	Amend/delay/reject legislative proposals Override veto Impeachment/trial Refuse to ratify treaties (Senate) Refuse to confirm appointments (Senate)
Congress on federal courts	Propose constitutional amendments Refuse to confirm appointments (Senate)
Federal courts on Congress	Declare law unconstitutional
Federal courts on president	Declare actions unconstitutional

20 A theory of government by which political power is divided between a national government and state governments, each having their own areas of substantive jurisdiction.

21 By:
- the enumerated powers of the federal government
- the implied powers of the federal government
- the concurrent powers of the federal and state governments
- the Tenth Amendment

22 (a) Any two of: economic stimulus package; expansion of S-CHIP; Medicaid; Obamacare.
(b) Any two of: ending Covid-19 lockdown; policies on illegal immigrants; using the national guard to police Black Lives Matter protests.

23 Any three of:
- Variation in state laws on such matters as age at which people can marry, drive a car, or have to attend school; the death penalty
- Federal and state courts
- States can act as policy laboratories, experimenting with new solutions to old problems
- All elections are state-based and run under state law
- Political parties in the USA are essentially decentralised, state-based parties
- Huge federal grants going to the states, as well as the complexity of the tax system because, for example, income tax is levied by both federal and some state governments
- The regions of the South, the Midwest, the Northeast and the West have distinct cultures as well as racial, religious and ideological differences

24 Any three of:
- Liberty
- Individualism
- Equality
- Representative government
- Limited government
- States' rights
- Gun ownership
- A fear of state-organised religion

25 Any three of:
- An autocratic monarchy
- The hereditary principle
- The power of a landed aristocracy
- An established church
- A deferential working class
- A lack of social mobility

26 Any three of:
- Primary elections
- Congressional committees
- The president's cabinet
- The Executive Office of the President
- The Supreme Court's power of judicial review

27 Acts of Parliament, common law, the works of Erskine May and Walter Bagehot.

28 Any three of:
- The powers, requirements and rights in the US Constitution are entrenched whereas those in the UK Constitution are not.
- The US Constitution allows for much more popular and democratic participation than does the UK Constitution.
- The US Constitution establishes a separation of powers whereas the UK Constitution establishes more in the way of fused powers, especially between the executive and the legislature.
- Checks and balances are more significant in the US Constitution than in the UK Constitution.
- The US Constitution enshrines the principle of federalism whereas the UK Constitution enshrines the principle of devolution.

Chapter 2

1 Two.

2 House: 435; Senate: 100.

3 House: proportional to state population; Senate: two per state.

4 Women: 118 in House; 24 in Senate. Black Americans: 55 in House; 3 in Senate. Hispanic/Latino: 45 in House; 5 in Senate. Asian: 19 in House; 2 in Senate.

5
- Between 2001 and the end of 2222, the House had been controlled by the Democrats for 8 years and the Republicans for 14 years.
- During the same period, the Senate had been controlled by the Republicans for just over 10.5 years and by the Democrats for just over 11.5 years.
- Only two of Congress's 535 members belong to neither party — senators Bernie Sanders (Vermont) and Angus King (Maine) — but both almost always vote with the Democrats.

6 Law making; oversight; confirmation of appointments.

7 A formal accusation of a serving federal official by a simple majority vote of the House of Representatives.

8 (a) simple majority; (b) two-thirds majority; (c) two-thirds majority.

9 Confirmation of appointments; ratification of treaties.

10 Any three of:
- Senators represent the entire state.
- Senators serve longer terms.
- Senators are one of only 100.
- Senators are more likely to chair a committee or sub-committee.
- The Senate is seen as a recruiting pool for the presidency and vice presidency.

11 Any three of:
- In passing legislation
- In conducting oversight of the executive
- In initiating constitutional amendments
- In fulfilling a representative function
- In receiving equal salaries

12 Any two of: Ted Cruz, Rand Paul, Marco Rubio, Rick Santorum, Lindsey Graham, Hillary Clinton, Bernie Sanders, Jim Webb.

13 Walter Mondale, Dan Quayle, Al Gore, Joe Biden, Mike Pence.

14 Standing committees, select committees, conference committees.

15 18 in the Senate, 30–40 in the House.

16 It reflects the party balance of each respective chamber.

17 They conduct the committee stage of bills; conduct investigations; begin confirmation process of appointments (Senate only).

18 Lloyd Austin, Anthony Blinkin, Janet Yellen, Merrick Garland.

19 It prioritises bills coming from the committee stage on to the floor of the House for their debate and votes by giving a 'rule' to a bill setting out the rules of debate, stating whether or not further amendments are permitted.

20 To reconcile the differences between the House and Senate versions of a bill.

21 When an investigation does not fall within the policy area of one standing committee, or when the investigation is likely to be particularly time consuming.

22 How legislators represent the views of their constituents; how representative legislators are of society as a whole in such matters as race and gender.

23 Trustee model: the legislator makes decisions on behalf of their constituents — the legislator acts as a 'trustee'. Delegate model: the legislator decides in accordance with the views of a majority of their constituents.

24 Any four of:
- Holding party and town hall meetings
- Conducting 'surgeries' with individual constituents
- Making visits around the state/district
- Appearing on local radio phone-ins
- Taking part in interviews with local media
- Addressing various groups in their state/district (e.g. chambers of commerce, Rotary clubs)
- Using email and social media

25 The committee stage is as far as most bills get; committees have full power of amendment; committees have life-and-death power over bills.

26 A device by which one or more senators can delay action on a bill or any other matter by debating it at length or through other obstructive actions.

27 Sign the bill; leave the bill on their desk; veto the bill.

28 (a) The president's power under Article II of the Constitution to return a bill to Congress unsigned, along with the reasons for his objection.

(b) A veto power exercised by the president at the end of a legislative session whereby bills not signed are lost.

29 Pass the bill again with a two-thirds majority in both houses.

30 Congressional review and investigation of the activities of the executive branch of government.

31 Any two of:
- Standing committee hearings
- The subpoena of documents and testimony
- The Senate's power to confirm appointments
- The Senate's power to ratify treaties

32 Because there are no executive branch members present in the legislature.

33 Any three of: political party; the administration; interest groups; colleagues and staff; personal beliefs.

34 Any three of: the president; the vice president; senior members of the White House staff; the president's congressional liaison staff; cabinet officers.

35 Almost all members are either Democrats or Republicans; the two major parties control all leadership positions.

36 Any two of:
- Era of 'hyper-partisanship'
- Greater unity within the parties, especially in the House (see Figure 2.1)
- More distinct conflicts between the parties
- Big-ticket items tend to pass on strictly party-line votes (e.g. President Trump's tax cuts in December 2017 received no Democrat votes in either house)
- Few 'centrists' left in Congress

37 (a) Partisanship: a situation where members of one party regularly group together to oppose members of another party, characterised by strong party discipline and little cooperation between the parties.

(b) Gridlock: failure to get action on policy proposals and legislation in Congress. Gridlock is thought to be exacerbated by divided government and partisanship.

38 Numbers have declined.
39 Party unity has increased significantly in the House over the past decade.
40 Any two of:
- Presence/absence of the executive
- Chief executive's relationship with the legislature
- Rules regarding removal
- Party ties/discipline

41 Similarities, any four of: both bicameral; different parties may control each house; chief executive may not control both houses; both houses have a role in legislation and oversight; committees are important; much oversight conducted by committees; all elections are first-past-the-post.

Differences, any four of, that in Congress: both houses are elected; both houses are equal; only two parties represented; executive branch excluded; two- and six-year terms of office; Senate only 100 members; Senate has significant oversight powers; each American has three representatives in Congress.

42 Congress, any two of: federalism; state-based representation; direct election.

Parliament, any two of: unitary/devolved structure of the UK; MPs represent parts of historic counties, cities or towns; hereditary principle — landed gentry, established church.

43 The differences concern (any four of): existence or not of a government programme; levels of party discipline; numbers of bills introduced — both total and by individual members; proportion of bills that become law; role of committee stage; nature of standing committees; whether bills are considered by the two chambers concurrently or consecutively; equality of the two chambers in passing legislation; existence of veto power.

44 Congress: standing committee hearings; select committee hearings; confirmation of appointments (Senate); ratification of treaties (Senate); impeachment, trial and removal from office.

Parliament: Question Time; selection committee hearings; Liaison Committee hearings; correspondence with ministers; early day motions; policy debates; Ombudsman; votes of no confidence.

45 Any four of: length of terms of office; number of parties; presence/absence of executive; relative powers compared with upper house; constituencies represented; legislative process; nature and role of standing committees; role of Speaker; onward movement of members to upper house.

46 Any four of: election/hereditary, appointed; number of members; terms of office; role of two major parties; legislative power; oversight powers; onward movement of members.

Chapter 3

1 They can propose, sign and veto legislation.
2 The State of the Union Address.
3 They appoint department and agency heads (e.g. Mike Pompeo); they appoint federal judges, including Supreme Court justices (e.g. Neil Gorsuch).
4 Acts as commander-in-chief of the armed forces; negotiates treaties.
5 On the same ticket as the president.
6 The president can appoint a replacement.
7 Voting in the case of a tied vote in the Senate; becoming president on the death, resignation or removal of the president.
8 The advisory group selected by the president to assist in making decisions and coordinating the work of the federal government.
9 Because they cannot be both in the cabinet and in Congress.
10 State governors, city mayors, academics, policy specialists.
11 In terms of gender, race, age, region, ideology.
12 Engender team spirit; promote collegiality; exchange information; debate/promote policy, especially 'big-ticket' items.
13 Get to know colleagues; resolve interdepartmental disputes; speak to the president.
14 The umbrella term for the top staff agencies in the White House that assist the president in carrying out the major responsibilities of office.
15 12.
16 Acts as liaison between the White House and the vast federal bureaucracy.
17 Any three of:
- The door-keeper of the Oval Office
- Decides whom the president sees, what they read, who speaks to them on the phone
- Should act as someone who sometimes takes the blame for the president if things go wrong
- Potentially the most powerful person in the White House after the president

18 Any two of:
- To advise the president on the allocation of federal funds in the annual budget
- To oversee the spending of all federal departments and agencies
- To act as a clearing house for all legislative and regulatory initiatives coming from the president

19 To help the president coordinate foreign, security and defence policy.
20 Any three of:
- The State Department
- The Defense Department
- The Central Intelligence Agency (CIA)
- The joint chiefs of staff
- US ambassadors around the world

21 Any three of:
- While EXOP members work in or near the West Wing, cabinet members work often some geographic distance from the White House.
- While key EXOP members may see the president on a regular basis, some members of the cabinet rarely get to see the president — and certainly not one on one.
- Therefore, while EXOP members often know what the president wants from day to day, cabinet members often feel out of the loop.
- While EXOP members work only for the president, cabinet members have divided loyalties — to the president, but also to Congress, to their bureaucracy and to client interest groups.
- EXOP staff therefore often regard cabinet members as being disloyal.

22 (a) Amend, delay or reject legislation; (b) override the veto by a two-thirds majority in both houses; (c) Senate must confirm; (d) Senate must ratify.

23 Any three of:
- The vice president
- The Office of Legislative Affairs (part of the White House Office)
- Cabinet officers
- Party leadership in Congress

24 Any three of:
- Phone calls
- Support legislation important to a member of Congress
- Invitations — social or political — to the White House
- Campaign for them (only for members from the president's party)
- Go on TV to appeal directly to voters and ask them to contact their members of Congress and tell them to support the president

25 'Bargainer-in-chief'.

26 An annual statistic that measures how often the president won in recorded votes in Congress on which the president took a clear position, expressed as a percentage of all such votes. Obama's score varied widely because the score tends to be higher in the first term and when the president's party controls both houses of Congress.

27 An official document issued by the executive branch with the effect of law, through which the president directs federal officials to take certain actions.

28 Because they are easy for a president to issue.

29 A statement issued by the president on signing a bill, which may challenge specific provisions of the bill on constitutional or other grounds.

30 Critics claim they are an abuse of presidential power over legislation; supporters see them as a way of the president getting their way over legislation even when Congress is uncooperative.

31 A temporary appointment of a federal official made by the president to fill a vacancy while the Senate is in recess.

32 Another way of the president getting their way against an uncooperative Congress — this time gridlock in the Senate over confirmation of appointments.

33 A presidency characterised by the misuse of presidential powers, particularly excessive secrecy — especially in foreign policy — and high-handedness in dealing with Congress. Associated with Richard Nixon.

34 A presidency characterised by ineffectiveness and weakness, resulting from congressional overassertiveness. Associated with Gerald Ford and Jimmy Carter.

35 Characterised by presidential re-assertiveness but power that is often limited by a new era of hyper-partisanship.

36 To act as commander-in-chief of the armed forces; to negotiate treaties with foreign powers; to make certain appointments, e.g. secretary of state, secretary of defense, director of the CIA, ambassadors.

37 Any three of:
- Declare war (but not used since 1941)
- Control the budget (including military spending)
- Ratify treaties (Senate only)
- Confirm appointments (Senate only)
- Investigate (through such committees as the Senate Foreign Relations Committee, the House Armed Services Committee)

38 Any three of:
- Amend, delay, reject the president's legislative proposals and budgetary requests
- Override the president's veto
- Refuse to ratify treaties (Senate)
- Refuse to confirm appointments (Senate)
- Investigate the president's actions and policies
- Impeach, try and remove the president from office

39 May declare the president's actions to be unconstitutional.

40 Any three of: public opinion; interest groups; voters; federal bureaucracy; state governments.

41 Any three of: electoral mandate; public approval; first/second term; unified/divided government; crises.

42 People tend to 'rally round the flag' and look to the president for leadership.

43 Any four of:
- The presidency is the product of revolution; the PM is the product of evolution.
- The president is elected by the people; the PM is elected as party leader by the party.
- The president is entirely separate from the legislature; the PM is a member of the legislature.
- The president is limited to two terms; there are no term limits for the PM.
- The president is aided by an advisory cabinet; the PM has a cabinet that is more than merely advisory.

- The president can be removed only by impeachment; the PM may be removed as leader by their party, or as a consequence of losing a confidence vote in the House of Commons.

44 Any four of:
- The president fulfils roles of head of state and chief executive; the PM is only chief executive.
- The president has formal input only at the start and finish of the legislative process; the PM draws up the government's legislative programme.
- The president appoints cabinet subject to Senate confirmation; the PM appoints cabinet without formal checks.
- The president acts as commander-in-chief but only Congress can declare war; the PM can use the royal prerogative to declare war and deploy troops abroad.
- The president has an elected VP, who automatically succeeds if the president dies, resigns or is removed from office; the PM may appoint an unofficial deputy PM.
- The president has a large EXOP; the PM has a small Number 10 staff plus Cabinet Office.
- The president submits annual budget to Congress, which forms the basis for negotiations with Congress; the PM submits annual budget to Parliament, which is usually passed without significant amendment.
- The president appoints all federal judges; the PM has no such power.
- The president has a pardon power; the PM has no such power.

45 The doctrine of the separation of powers — that the president is entirely separate from Congress.

46 Because of the significant differences in powers, role, membership, meetings, relationship with president/PM.

Chapter 4

1 Nine.

2 The president.

3 By the Senate, simple majority required.

4 For life, or until they voluntarily retire.

5 Voluntary resignation, removal through impeachment, or death.

6 Strict constructionist: a Supreme Court justice who interprets the Constitution strictly or literally and tends to stress the retention of power by individual states. Loose constructionist: a Supreme Court justice who interprets the Constitution less literally and tends to stress the broad grants of power to the federal government.

7 Strict: Roberts, Thomas, Alito, Gorsuch, Kavanaugh. Loose: Breyer, Sotomayor, Kagan.

8 Swing justice.

9 A Supreme Court justice who interprets the Constitution in line with the meaning or intent of the framers at the time of enactment.

10 They would consider the Constitution as a dynamic, living document, interpretation of which should take account of the views of contemporary society.

11 The five-stage process is:
- A vacancy occurs.
- The president instigates a search for possible nominees and interviews short-listed candidates.
- The president announces their nominee.
- The Senate Judiciary Committee holds a confirmation hearing on the nominee and makes a recommendatory vote.
- The nomination is debated and voted on in the full Senate. A simple majority vote is required for confirmation.

12 Voting is now usually along party lines.

13 Any three of:
- Presidents have tended to politicise the nominations by attempting to choose justices who share their political views and judicial philosophy (e.g. Obama with Kagan; Trump with Gorsuch).
- The Senate has tended to politicise the confirmation process by focusing more on hot-button issues (e.g. women's rights) than on qualifications.
- Members of the Senate Judiciary Committee from the president's party tend to ask soft questions of the nominee.
- Members of the Senate Judiciary Committee from the opposition party attempt, through their questions, to attack or embarrass the nominee rather than to elicit relevant information.
- Justices are now frequently confirmed on party-line votes (e.g. Gorsuch).
- The media conduct a 'feeding frenzy' often connected with matters of trivia.

14 Any three of:
- They occur infrequently.
- They are for life.
- Just one new appointee to a nine-member body can significantly change its philosophical balance.
- The Supreme Court has the power of judicial review.
- Their decisions will profoundly affect the lives of ordinary Americans for generations to come.

15 The power of the Supreme Court to declare Acts of Congress, actions of the executive, or Acts or actions of state governments unconstitutional.

16 It was 'found' by the Court in *Marbury* v *Madison* (1803) — regarding a federal law — and used again in *Fletcher* v *Peck* (1810) — regarding a state law.

17 Because the effects of its decisions have almost the effect of a law having been passed by Congress.

18 An approach to judicial decision making that holds that judges should use their position to promote desirable social ends, even if that means overturning the decisions of elected officials.

19 Any two of:
- *Roe* v *Wade* (1973) — guaranteed a woman's right to choose an abortion.

- *District of Columbia* v *Heller* (2008) — guaranteed individual gun ownership rights.
- *Obergefell* v *Hodges* (2015) — guaranteed rights to same-sex marriage.

20 An approach to judicial decision making that holds that judges should defer to the legislative and executive branches, and to precedent established in previous Court decisions.

21 A legal principle that judges should look to past precedents as a guide wherever possible (literally, 'let the decision stand').

22 Any two of:
- *Zelman* v *Simmons-Harris* (2002) — the Court upheld an Ohio state programme giving financial aid to parents, allowing them, if they so chose, to send their children to a religious or private school. Significance: state government money could be finding its way to a religious, private school.
- *Town of Greece* v *Galloway* (2014) — the Court allowed legislative bodies (such as town councils) to begin their meetings with prayer. Significance: strengthened individual rights to practise religion in public, even in state-constituted and state-funded bodies.
- *Burwell* v *Hobby Lobby Stores Inc.* (2010) — the Court overturned the requirement under the Affordable Care Act (2010) (otherwise known as Obamacare) that family-owned firms had to pay for health insurance coverage for contraception as this violated the religious beliefs of some Christian-run companies. Significance: strengthened individual rights of Christian business executives to run their companies along lines that agreed with their religious beliefs.

23 Any two of:
- *McConnell* v *Federal Election Commission* (2004) — upheld federal law (Bipartisan Campaign Reform Act) banning soft money in election campaigns, stating that this ban did not violate freedom of speech. Significance: limiting campaign finance is not incompatible with the freedom of speech provision of the Constitution.
- *Citizens United* v *FEC* (2010) — ruled that when it comes to rights of political speech, business corporations and labour unions have the same rights as individuals. Significance: opened the door to unlimited spending by corporations in election campaigns, mostly funnelled through PACs.
- *McCutcheon* v *FEC* (2014) — the Court struck down a 1970s limit on totals that wealthy individuals can contribute to candidates and PACs. Significance: reaffirmed giving of money to candidates and PACs as a fundamental right.

24 Never before had the courts ruled this interpretation of the Second Amendment.

25 The Court was clearly seen as telling us what eighteenth-century words mean in the twenty-first-century USA.

26 Any two of:
- *Roe* v *Wade* (1973) — ruled that the state law of Texas forbidding abortion was unconstitutional. Significance: guaranteed a woman's right to choose an abortion as a constitutionally protected right.
- *Gonzales* v *Carhart* (2007) — upheld the Partial Birth Abortion Act (2003), which banned late-term abortions. Significance: established that a woman's right to choose an abortion could be legally limited.
- *Whole Woman's Health* v *Hellerstedt* (2016) — struck down as unconstitutional two parts of a Texas state law concerning abortion provision. Significance: not all limits on a woman's right to choose would be regarded as constitutionally permissible.

27 Any two of:
- *United States* v *Windsor* (2013) — declared the Defense of Marriage Act (1996) to be unconstitutional and that it is unconstitutional to treat same-sex married couples differently from other married couples in terms of federal benefits.
- *Obergefell* v *Hodges* (2015) — declared that state bans on same-sex marriage were unconstitutional.

28 Examples might include *National Federation of Independent Business* v *Sebelius* (2012); *United States* v *Stevens* (2010); *United States* v *Citizens United* (2010).

29 *National Labor Relations Board* v *Noel Canning* (2014).

30 Any two of:
- The Senate has the power to confirm or reject appointments.
- Congress fixes the numerical size of the Court.
- Congress has the power of impeachment — even the threat of impeachment is a check.
- Congress can initiate constitutional amendments that would have the effect of overturning the Court's decision.

31 The president has the power to nominate justices; can decide whether or not to throw political weight behind a decision of the Court, thereby either enhancing or decreasing the Court's perceived legitimacy.

32 Any two of:
- The Court has no power of initiation: it must wait for cases to be brought before it.
- The Court has no enforcement powers: it is dependent on the other branches of government and/or the rule of law for implementation of and obedience to Court decisions.
- Public opinion: if the Court makes decisions that are regarded as wrong by a majority of the public, the Court loses some of its legitimacy.
- The Court is checked by itself — by decisions it has already made.
- The Court is checked by the Constitution — although certain parts of the Constitution are open to the Court's interpretation, other parts are very specific.

33 US Supreme Court created by Founding Fathers in 1787; UK Supreme Court created by Act of Parliament in 2009. US Supreme Court written into the Constitution; UK Supreme Court written into Act of Parliament. US Supreme Court was the first federal court to be created; UK Supreme Court was the last UK court to be created.
34 US system is based on 'separated institutions, sharing powers' while the UK system is based on 'fused powers'. US system was the product of revolution while the UK system is the product of evolution.
35 USA: nominated by the president and confirmed by the Senate. UK: nominated by the Judicial Appointments Commission (no confirmation required).
36 USA: life tenure. UK: must retire at 70 if appointed after 1995, otherwise must retire at 75.
37 Latin phrase (literally, 'beyond the powers') used to describe an action that is beyond one's legal power or authority. It is important in the UK Supreme Court because it centres on the Court's tendency to declare the actions of ministers *ultra vires*.
38 The executive, the legislature, the media.
39 Any two of: judges' immunity from prosecution for acts carried out as judges; immunity from lawsuits of defamation for what they say while hearing cases; salaries cannot be reduced.

Chapter 5

1 Civil rights: positive acts of government designed to protect people against arbitrary or discriminatory treatment by government or individuals.

Civil liberties: those liberties, mostly spelt out in the Constitution, that guarantee the protection of people, expression and property from arbitrary interference by government.

2 Any three of: legislation; constitutional amendment; decision of the Supreme Court; presidential leadership; citizen action.
3 Rights of the physically disabled by the Americans with Disabilities Act (1990); gay rights by *Obergefell* v *Hodges* (2015).
4 A programme giving members of a previously disadvantaged minority group a head start in, for example, higher education or employment.
5 The mandated movement of school children between racially homogeneous neighbourhoods — white suburbs and black inner cities — to create racially mixed schools.
6 A programme by which a certain percentage (quota) of places in, for example, higher education or employment is reserved for people from previously disadvantaged minorities.
7 Equality of opportunity focuses on giving the same rights and opportunities to all. Equality of results focuses on outcomes — on giving advantages to previously disadvantaged groups.
8 Any two of: *Gratz* v *Bollinger* (2003); *Grutter* v *Bollinger* (2003); *Parents Involved* v *Seattle School District* (2007); *Fisher* v *University of Texas* (2013 and 2016).
9 Advantages — any three of:
- Leads to greater levels of diversity
- Rights previous wrongs — those previously disadvantaged are now advantaged
- Opens up areas of education and employment that otherwise would be out of the reach of disadvantaged minorities
- In education, creates a more diverse student body, thereby promoting integration and racial tolerance

Disadvantages — any three of:
- Advantage for one group leads to disadvantage for other groups — 'reverse discrimination'
- Can lead to minorities being admitted to higher education courses and jobs with which they are ill equipped to cope
- Can be condescending to minorities
- Perpetuates a society based on colour and race

10 Any two of:
- Legislation, e.g. Voting Rights Act (1965) and the re-authorisation of key parts of this Act in 2006
- Voter registration drives among black and Hispanic communities
- Voter turnout drives among the same groups

11 Either introduction by some states of photo ID requirement at polling stations, or removal of voting rights following criminal convictions.
12 Black members up from 16 in 1979–80 to 49 in 2017–18; Hispanic/Latino members up from 6 in 1979–80 to 38 in 2017–18.
13 Any two of: Ben Carson, Bobby Jindal, Marco Rubio.
14 10 women; 8 of minority ethnicity.
15 Got Congress to pass the Development, Relief, and Education for Alien Minors (DREAM) Act. Also created the DACA programme.
16 Deferred Action for Childhood Arrivals (2012), which allowed some individuals who entered the country as the children of illegal immigrants to have the temporary right to live, study and work in the USA.
17 Announced his intention to end the DACA programme, make the deportation of all illegal immigrants a top priority, and build a wall along the USA–Mexico border. He was successful with closing DACA but only managed to build a small section of the wall.
18 In the USA, rights are entrenched in a codified constitution.
19 The Constitution, Acts of Congress, decisions of the Supreme Court.
20 Acts of Parliament, decisions of the courts.
21 Supporters of same-sex marriage and orthodox Christians.
22 Effective protection of rights versus the need for security.
23 In the USA: ACLU and NAACP; in the UK: Liberty and Stonewall.

Chapter 6

1 Every four years.
2 A natural-born US citizen; at least 35 years of age; resident in the USA for at least 14 years.
3 Limits presidents to two full terms in office.
4 The period between candidates declaring an intention to run for the presidency and the first primaries and caucuses.
5 The calendar year before the presidential election.
6 Any three of:
   - Candidate announcements
   - Televised party debates
   - Fundraising
   - Raising national name recognition for lesser-known candidates
   - Opinion polls showing who are the front-runners
   - Endorsements by leading party figures (e.g. members of Congress, state governors, former presidents)
7 A primary is an election; a caucus is a meeting.
8 Show popularity of presidential candidates; choose delegates to go to the national party conventions.
9 (a) A Tuesday in February or early March when a number of states coincide their presidential primaries and caucuses to try to gain influence.
   (b) The phenomenon by which states schedule their primaries or caucuses earlier in the nomination cycles in an attempt to increase their importance.
10 Open primary: any registered voter may vote in either primary. Closed primary: only registered Republicans can vote in the Republican primary and only registered Democrats can vote in the Democratic primary.
11 Proportional primary: delegates are awarded to candidates in proportion to the votes they get. Winner-take-all primary: the winner of the popular vote wins all the delegates.
12 Primaries and caucuses are still held but little attention is given to them.
13 Turnout is low: 20–30% on average in primaries; much lower in caucuses.
14 (a) Reasons why they are important — any three of:
   - The presidential candidates emerge during them.
   - A large number of candidates are eliminated by them.
   - Delegates (who make the final decision about the candidate) are chosen by them.
   - They attract a large amount of media attention.
   - Lesser-known candidates see them as a way of boosting name recognition.
   - They test some presidential skills (e.g. oratorical, presentational, organisational).
   - They are much more important than they used to be before the McGovern–Fraser reforms (1970s).

   (b) Reasons why they are not important — any three of:
   - Primaries often merely confirm decisions made during the 'invisible primary' (i.e. the candidates leading in the polls at the start of the primaries are the ones eventually chosen).
   - What goes on in the media (e.g. televised candidate debates) is often more important.
   - Many presidential skills are not tested (e.g. ability to compromise, ability to work with Congress).
   - Many primaries choose so few delegates that they cannot be regarded as important.
15 (a) Strengths — any three of:
   - Increased levels of participation by voters
   - Increased choice of candidates
   - Process opened up to outside candidates (e.g. Obama, Trump)
   - A gruelling race for a gruelling job

   (b) Weaknesses — any three of:
   - Can lead to voter apathy
   - Voters are often unrepresentative
   - Process is too long, too expensive, too dominated by the media
   - Can develop into bitter personal battles
   - Lack of 'peer review'
   - Role of 'super-delegates' (Democrats)
16 Choosing the presidential candidate; choosing the vice presidential candidate; deciding the party platform.
17 Promoting party unity; enthusing the party faithful; enthusing ordinary voters.
18 (a) Are important — any three of:
   - The only time the national parties meet together
   - Provide an opportunity to promote party unity after the primaries
   - Provide an opportunity to enthuse the party faithful to go and campaign for the ticket
   - Introduce the presidential candidates to the public
   - Delivery of the acceptance speech
   - Can lead to a significant 'bounce' in the polls
   - Many voters don't tune in to the campaign until the conventions start
   - A significant number of voters make their decision about whom to vote for at this stage

   (b) Are not important — any three of:
   - Nowadays they make few (if any) significant decisions; merely confirm decisions made earlier that we already know about
   - Television coverage has become much reduced
   - Ordinary voters don't really see them as important
   - Those held when the party is nominating the sitting president for re-election can be pretty devoid of any real significance
   - More balloons, hoopla and celebrities than serious policy debate and presentation

19 Labor Day (first Monday in September).

20 Nine weeks.

21 An event occurring late in the presidential campaign to the disadvantage of one candidate, leaving that candidate with little or no time to recover before Election Day.

22 A political committee that raises limited amounts of money and spends contributions for the express purpose of electing or defeating candidates.

23 Any three of:
- National party committees banned from raising or spending 'soft money'
- Labour unions and corporations forbidden from directly funding issue ads
- Unions and corporations forbidden from financing ads that mention a federal candidate within 60 days of a general election or 30 days of a primary
- Increased individual limits on contributions to individual candidates or candidate committees
- Banned contributions from foreign nationals
- Provided for a 'stand by your ad' verbal endorsement by candidates on TV ads

24 Commission on Presidential Debates.

25 Podiums, town hall, round table.

26 Any three of:
- Can play a decisive role in the campaign (e.g. 1980, 2012)
- Can affect the opinion polls
- Especially important for the challenging candidate who will be less well known
- A good sound bite from a candidate will be played repeatedly in the media in the days that follow
- A gaffe can seriously affect a candidate's chances of success (e.g. Gore in 2000)

27 Any three of:
- In 2016, polls found that Clinton easily won all three debates, yet she lost the election.
- Trump's numerous debate gaffes did not seriously affect his poll numbers.
- Policy detail is rarely discussed.
- They are not really 'debates', more the trotting out of rehearsed lines and catchphrases.
- Viewership has tended to decline (though it was up in 2016).

28 Fixed as the Tuesday after the first Monday in November.

29 More than 30.

30 Dropped steadily from 1960 to 1996, then increased in 2000–08, fell again in 2016, but increased significantly to 67% in 2020.

31 Four: Gerald Ford, Jimmy Carter, George H.W. Bush, Donald Trump.

32 Equal to each state's representation in Congress.

33 270.

34 Winner-take-all.

35 Maine and Nebraska: winner in each congressional district wins one electoral vote; the state-wide winner wins the remaining two electoral votes.

36 An Elector in the Electoral College who casts their ballot for a candidate other than the one who won the popular vote in their state. See Table 6.7 for examples.

37 Preserves the voice of the small-population states; usually results in a two-horse race.

38 Any four of:
- Small-population states are over-represented
- Winner-take-all system can distort the result
- Possible for the loser of the popular vote to win the Electoral College vote
- Unfair to national third parties
- 'Rogue' or 'faithless' Electors
- Potential problem if Electoral College is deadlocked

39 Direct election; congressional district system; proportional system.

40 National Popular Vote Interstate Compact — an agreement to cast all Electoral College votes to the winner of the popular vote. Could change the identity of the winner, e.g. Clinton would have been made president in 2016 if the NPVIC had been in operation then.

41 Any two of:
- There is no widespread consensus on a better alternative
- Highly unlikely that any significant reform would be legislatively or constitutionally achievable
- The suggested reforms also have significant problems

42 All of the House; one-third of the Senate.

43 Elections for the whole of the House and one-third of the Senate that occur midway through a president's four-year term.

44 By minimum age (House 25, Senate 30); by length of citizenship (House 7 years, Senate 9 years).

45 A state law that requires House members to be resident in the congressional district they represent.

46 Any two of:
- Their ability to provide federal funding for constituency/state projects
- High levels of name recognition
- Fundraising advantages — incumbents can usually raise much more than challengers can

47 The effect when an extremely popular candidate at the top of the ticket (e.g. for president or governor) carries candidates for lower offices with them into office.

48 Voting for candidates of the same party for different offices at the same election.

49 Any two of:
- It makes it much harder for party control of the House to change hands.
- Members from safe districts are more likely to cast party-line votes than are those from competitive ones.
- It therefore increases levels of partisanship.

50 Without the winning presidential candidate on the ticket, House members from the president's party do less well; voters see the midterms as an opportunity to express disappointment/disapproval with the president.

Chapter 7

1 Federalism.

2 National committee, national chair, national convention.

3 Any three of:
- New campaign finance laws resulted in money flowing to the national parties and the candidates themselves rather than being raised by the state or local parties.
- Television provided a medium through which candidates could appeal directly to voters, thereby cutting out state and local parties that had traditionally been the medium.
- Emergence of sophisticated opinion polls allowed candidates to 'hear' directly what voters were saying without actually meeting them.
- New technology allowed national parties to set up sophisticated fundraising and direct mailing operations — later also via social media.
- Parties became more ideologically cohesive.
- National parties played a larger role in recruitment and training of congressional candidates.

4 The national chairs.

5 State, congressional district, county, city, ward, precinct.

6 A collectively held set of beliefs.

7 Democrats = liberal; Republicans = conservative.

8 Social conservatives focus on issues such as abortion and same-sex marriage; fiscal conservatives focus on issues such as the national debt, federal budget deficit and taxation.

9 Any four of:
- Increased spending on social welfare programmes
- Death penalty
- Gun control
- High levels of defence spending
- Stricter environmental controls
- Stricter controls on immigration
- 'Obamacare'

10 The Democratic Party.

11 The Republican Party.

12 Any four of: small town/rural, conservatives, white, men, over 65, 45–64, high-school-only educated.

13 Any four of: black people, liberals, Hispanics, Asians, city, 18–29, women, earning less than $30,000.

14 The gap between the support given to a candidate by women and the support given to the same candidate by men.

15 The Democrats tend to take policy positions more favoured by women on (any three of):
- Abortion rights (support)
- Capital punishment (oppose)
- Gun control (support)
- Lower levels of defence spending (support)

16 Any three of:
- They felt neglected by Washington politicians of both parties who had made promises to them during campaigns but had failed to deliver once elected.
- The effects of the 2008–09 economic crash — they believed that whereas the government bailed out banks and big business, they were left unemployed and not helped.
- They believed that their values, way of life and beliefs (e.g. in traditional marriage) had been swept aside and sneered at by a 'liberal elite'.
- They felt that the USA in which they grew up — overwhelmingly white and nominally Christian — was fast disappearing.

17 His 'Make America Great Again' theme.

18 Any three of: Ohio, Florida, Virginia, North Carolina.

19 Protestants and those who attend places of worship regularly tend to vote Republican; Catholics and those who attend places of worship rarely tend to vote Democrat.

20 Any five of:
- Predominantly white
- Overwhelmingly Protestant (and especially evangelical)
- Rural, small town or suburban
- Fiscally and socially conservative
- Pro-guns
- Pro-life
- Pro-traditional marriage
- Support limited role for federal government
- Opposed to Obamacare
- Watch Fox News

21 Any five of:
- A racial rainbow of white, black, Asian, Hispanic/Latino
- Urban
- Socially liberal
- Support gun control measures
- Pro-choice
- Pro-gay rights
- Support an expansive role for federal government
- Support Obamacare
- Watch CNN and *Saturday Night Live*

22 Any three of:
- They lost the presidential election in 2016 — though their candidate won nearly 3 million more votes than her opponent.
- From 2008 to 2016 they lost 10 seats in the Senate and 61 in the House, losing control of both chambers.
- During the same period the number of Democrat governors fell from 29 to 16.
- They lost nearly 1,000 state legislative seats during the same eight-year period.
- At state level, the party in 2017 was at its lowest electoral level since 1925.

23 Conflict between the liberal wing and the establishment wing.

24 Tea Party, Freedom Caucus, establishment versus Trump.

25 A party system in which two major parties regularly win the vast majority of the votes, capture nearly all of the seats in the legislature and alternately control the executive.

26 Any three of:
- Popular vote — in all the last seven presidential elections, the two major parties have won more than 80% of the popular vote, on four occasions exceeding 95%.
- Congressional seats — after 2016, the two major parties controlled 533 of the 535 seats in Congress.
- Executive branch control — every president since 1853 has been a Democrat or a Republican.
- State government — by 2017, 49 of the 50 state governors were either Democrats or Republicans.

27 Electoral system; broad party ideologies; primary elections.

28 National (Libertarian Party, Green Party); regional (American Independence Party in 1968); state (New York Conservative Party).

29 Any two of:
- Might be thought to have little or no impact as they rarely win a significant number of votes.
- But might be thought to have some significant impact in that they can:
  - influence the outcome even with a very small percentage of the votes (e.g. 2000)
  - influence the policy agenda of the two major parties (e.g. the Green Party)
- Third parties can have some impact within certain states.

30 Any three of:
- Electoral system: first-past-the-post, winner-take-all system makes it very difficult for third parties to win.
- Ballot access laws: third parties are disadvantaged by laws regulating how candidates must qualify for the ballot in each of the 50 states.
- Lack of resources: difficulties in raising significant amounts of money result in little to spend on campaigning, advertising, organisation, get-out-the-vote operations.
- Lack of media coverage: not newsworthy; cannot afford TV advertising; excluded from TV debates.
- Co-optation of their policies: major parties may co-opt their policies, thereby depriving them of future success.

31 USA: federal matching funds; UK: Short money.

32 Arguments for — any three of:
- End parties' dependence on wealthy donors
- Enable parties better to perform their democratic functions — organisation, representation, creating policy priorities
- Fill the gap created by falling membership
- Lead to greater transparency
- Help equalise parties' financial resources
- Make it easier to limit spending
- Encourage greater public engagement if funding were linked to electoral turnout

Arguments against — any three of:
- Reinforce the financial advantage of major parties
- Further increase disconnect between parties and voters
- Diminish belief in the principle that citizen participation is voluntary
- Lead to objections from taxpayers whose money would go to parties they don't support
- Reinforce the parties' role, which many see as an anachronism in the digital age

33 The rise of nationalism in Scotland, Wales and Northern Ireland.

34 Any three of:
- To accentuate certain policies
- To focus on a particular ideological aspect
- To reflect geographic, ethnic, economic, generational, religious groups
- To widen voter appeal
- To extol the party 'greats'
- To challenge the party establishment

35 Any three of:
- Dislike big government
- Favour low taxation
- Strong on law and order
- High levels of defence spending
- Focus on equality of opportunity rather than equality of results

36 Any three of:
- Rights of minorities
- Rights of workers
- Green policies
- Equality of results
- High levels of government spending on social welfare and education
- Higher levels of tax for the wealthy to fund services for the poor

37 Any three of:
- Abortion
- Death penalty
- Same-sex marriage
- Renewable energy
- National healthcare
- Role of central government in education

38 Groups that seek to represent their own section or group within society.

39 Any three of: business/trade; labour; agricultural; societal; professional; intergovernmental. See Table 7.4 for examples.

40 Groups that campaign for a particular cause or issue.

41 Any three of: single-interest; ideological; policy; think-tanks. See Table 7.5 for examples.

42 Any three of: representation; citizen participation; public education; agenda building; programme monitoring.

43 Electioneering/endorsing; lobbying; organising grassroots activities.

44 Any three of: environmental protection; women's rights; abortion; gun control.

45 Any two of:
- By directly lobbying members of Congress; attempting to influence legislation and the way members cast their votes
- By lobbying congressional committees, especially those who chair or are ranking minority members on relevant committees (see Chapter 2)
- By organising constituents — by phone, the internet and social media
- By publicising members' voting records and endorsing or opposing candidates

46 Seek to maintain strong ties with relevant executive departments, agencies and bureaus; seek to influence the drawing up of and enactment of policy within their area of interest.

47 Any two of:
- Take a lively interest in the nomination and confirmation of judges to the federal courts, especially those to the Supreme Court
- The American Bar Association (ABA) evaluates the professional qualifications of nominees
- Try to influence court hearings through *amicus curiae* (friend of the court) briefings, thereby presenting their views to the court in writing before oral arguments are heard
- One of the most influential groups is the American Civil Liberties Union (ACLU) which has helped bring high-profile cases to the courts over such issues as protecting affirmative action, and more recently on the issue of transgender rights

48 The practice by which former members of Congress (or the executive) take up well-paid jobs with Washington-based lobbying firms, using their expertise and contacts to lobby their previous institution.

49 A strong relationship between interest groups, the relevant congressional committees and the relevant government department, which attempts to achieve mutually beneficial policy outcomes.

50 Far more elective posts in the USA.

51 Congressional parties tend to be weaker.

52 More likely to be effective as Parliament is very party dominated.

53 The judiciary in the USA has greater political importance.

54 Any four of:
- Size of membership
- Amount of money available
- The group's strategic position in the political system
- The balance of public opinion
- Strength or weakness of countervailing group(s)
- Attitude of the administration (USA)/government (UK)
- Ability to access the media

Glossary

Term	Definition	Page(s)
Affirmative action	A programme giving members of a previously disadvantaged minority group a head-start in, for example, higher education or employment.	72
Balanced ticket	A pairing of presidential and vice presidential candidates on a ticket, who attract support for different reasons, thereby making the broadest appeal to voters.	82
Bipartisanship	Agreement or cooperation between two different political parties that usually oppose each other.	15
Busing	The mandated movement of school children between racially homogeneous neighbourhoods — white suburbs and black inner cities — to create racially mixed schools.	72
Cabinet	The advisory group selected by the president to assist in making decisions and coordinating the work of the federal government.	72
Campaign finance	The raising and spending of money to support a candidate or a political party in an election campaign.	84
Caucuses	A state-based series of meetings to choose a party's candidate for the presidency. They usually attract unrepresentative and low turnouts.	80
Checks and balances	A system of government that gives each branch — legislative, executive and judicial — the means partially to control the power exercised by the other branches.	13
Civil liberties	Those liberties, mostly spelt out in the Constitution, that guarantee the protection of people, expression and property from arbitrary interference by government.	71
Civil rights	Positive acts of government designed to protect people against arbitrary or discriminatory treatment by government or individuals.	71
Cloture motion	A vote to bring about the end of a filibuster, requiring a supermajority of senators in order to succeed.	29
Coattails effect	When an extremely popular candidate at the top of the ticket (e.g. for president or governor) carries candidates for lower offices with them into office.	91
Codification	The process of arranging rules or processes in written format.	9
Codified constitution	A constitution that consists of a full and authoritative set of rules written down in a single document.	10
Congressional caucuses	Also called 'conferences', congressional caucuses are groups of politicians who share the same interests and views, usually from the same political party.	26
Conservative justices	Justices with a narrow view of the Constitution. A term usually used to refer to strict constructionists who try to interpret the Constitution in a literal rather than loose manner.	64
Constitution	A set of political principles by which a country or organisation is governed.	9
Constitutional rights	Those individual rights provided and protected by the US Constitution.	71
Divided government	Where control of the executive branch (presidency) and the legislature (Congress) is split between two parties (e.g. when there is a Republican president but a Democrat majority in both the House and Senate).	34
Domestic politics	The decisions and policies that the executive and legislature make that are specifically to do with issues or events within a country.	40
Electoral College	The institution established by the Founding Fathers to elect the president and vice president indirectly. The Electors cast their ballots in their state capitals.	87
Electoral mandate	The size of the majority won by the president at the election — the higher the majority, the bigger the electoral mandate.	42
Entrenchment	The application of extra legal safeguards to a constitutional provision to make it more difficult to amend or abolish.	11

Term	Definition	Page(s)
Enumerated powers	Powers given to the federal government by the US Constitution.	10
Executive agreement	An agreement reached between the president and a foreign nation on matters that do not require a formal treaty.	49
Executive branch	The branch of government that has responsibility for exercising authority across the governed territory and for implementing and enforcing the laws created by the legislative branch.	40
Executive Office of the President (EXOP)	The umbrella term for the top staff agencies in the White House that assist the president in carrying out the major responsibilities of office.	44
Executive order	An official document issued by the executive branch with the effect of law, through which the president directs federal officials to take certain actions.	48
Federalism	A theory of government by which political power is divided between a national government and state governments, each having their own areas of substantive jurisdiction.	14
Filibuster	A device by which one or more senators can delay action on a bill or any other matter by debating it at length or through other obstructive actions.	29
Front loading	The phenomenon by which states schedule their primaries or caucuses earlier in the nomination cycles in an attempt to increase their importance.	80
Gender gap	The gap between the support given to a candidate by women and the support given to the same candidate by men.	96
Grassroots activity	Collective action at the local level.	109
Gridlock	Failure to get action on policy proposals and legislation in Congress. Gridlock is thought to be exacerbated by divided government and partisanship.	32
Hard money	Money given directly to a candidate to assist in his or her election campaign.	85
Ideology	A collectively held set of beliefs.	94
Impeachment	A formal accusation of serious wrongdoing or misconduct of a serving federal official by a simple majority vote of the House of Representatives.	14
Imperial judiciary	A term used by critics to describe an activist judiciary that allegedly exceeds its constitutional powers and attempts to overrule federal or state law rather than interpret the law. The term is used to criticise unelected judges having too much power.	61
Imperial presidency	A presidency characterised by the misuse of presidential powers, especially excessive secrecy — particularly in foreign policy — and high-handedness in dealing with Congress.	49
Imperilled presidency	A term coined by President Gerald Ford to refer to a presidency characterised by ineffectiveness and weakness, resulting from congressional over-assertiveness.	49
Incumbency	The holding of an office, position or role.	21
Incumbent	A person who currently holds an office.	21, 81
Informal powers	Political rather than constitutional powers.	42
Interpretative amendment	The ability of the Supreme Court to interpret the Constitution and, in effect, change the meaning of words within it.	12
Invisible primary	The period between candidates declaring an intention to run for the presidency and the first primaries and caucuses.	78
Iron-triangle syndrome	A strong relationship between interest groups, the relevant congressional committees and the relevant government department, which attempts to achieve mutually beneficial policy outcomes.	107
Judicial activism	An approach to judicial decision making that holds that judges should use their position to promote desirable social ends, even if that means overturning the decisions of elected officials.	61
Judicial restraint	An approach to judicial decision making that holds that judges should defer to the legislative and executive branches, and to precedent established in previous Court decisions.	61

Term	Definition	Page(s)
Judicial review	The power of the Supreme Court to declare Acts of Congress, actions of the executive, or Acts or actions of state governments unconstitutional.	60
Liberal justice	A Supreme Court justice who is usually a loose constructionist and generally interprets the Constitution in ways that give people more freedom.	58
Limited government	A government prevented from being all-powerful by the limits provided by the Constitution.	16
Living Constitution	The Constitution considered as a dynamic, living document, interpretation of which should take account of the views of contemporary society.	58
Locality rule	A state law that requires House members to be resident in the congressional district they represent.	90
Loose constructionist	A Supreme Court justice who interprets the Constitution less literally and tends to stress the broad grants of power to the federal government.	58
Midterm elections	Elections for the whole of the House and one-third of the Senate that occur midway through a president's four-year term.	21, 90
National party convention	The meeting held every four years by each of the two major parties to select presidential and vice presidential candidates and to agree the party platform.	83
October surprise	An event occurring late in the presidential campaign to the disadvantage of one candidate, leaving them with little or no time to recover before Election Day.	84
Originalism	Where a Supreme Court justice interprets the Constitution in line with the meaning or intent of the framers at the time of enactment.	58
Oversight	Congressional review and investigation of the activities of the executive branch of government.	29
Partisanship	A situation where members of one party regularly group together to oppose members of another party, characterised by strong party discipline and little cooperation between the parties.	32
Party factions	A group or groups within a single political party that share views and interests that are different from the rest of the party.	102
Party system	How a political system focused through political parties is organised.	93
Pocket veto	A veto power exercised by the president at the end of a legislative session whereby bills not signed are lost.	29
Policy groups	Interest groups which have a wide range of proposed policies that they hope government will implement (e.g. the Sierra Club is an environmental interest group which develops policy in a wide range of areas affecting the environment).	105
Political action committee (PAC)	A political committee that raises limited amounts of money and spends these contributions for the express purpose of electing or defeating candidates.	84
Powers of persuasion	Using personal influence to convince others to provide support.	42
Presidential veto	The president's power under Article II of the Constitution to return a bill to Congress unsigned, along with the reasons for the objection.	29
Primary	A state-based election to choose a party's candidate for the presidency by showing support for candidates among ordinary voters. Primaries also select delegates to represent the state party at the national party conventions.	80
Professional groups	Interest groups which represent certain occupational or professional sectors (e.g. doctors, lawyers, teachers).	104
Public policy	Action enacted by government to deal with issues or problems affecting the public at large (e.g. education policy).	63
Quotas	A programme by which a certain percentage (quota) of places in, for example, higher education or employment is reserved for people from previously disadvantaged minorities.	72
Racial equality	When people of all races and ethnic backgrounds have equal access to services, institutions, rights and freedoms.	71
Ratify	To sign and give official consent to a change or amendment.	11

Term	Definition	Page(s)
Recess appointment	A temporary appointment of a federal official made by the president to fill a vacancy while the Senate is in recess.	48
Religious Right	A faction of the Republican Party which supports strongly conservative policies. They attempt to influence policy making and politics in general from a fundamentalist Christian point of view. They advocate, for example, pro-life policies, prayer in school and capital punishment.	94
Representation	Either how legislators represent their constituents or who the legislators are and whether they are 'representative' of constituents in terms of, for example, gender and race.	27
Revolving-door syndrome	The practice by which former members of Congress (or the executive) take up well-paid jobs with Washington-based lobbying firms, using their expertise and contacts to lobby their previous institution.	107
Rogue/faithless Elector	An Elector in the Electoral College who casts their ballot for a candidate other than the one who won the popular vote in their state.	87
Separation of powers	A theory of government whereby political power is distributed among the legislature, the executive and the judiciary, each acting both independently and interdependently.	13
Signing statement	A statement issued by the president on signing a bill which may challenge specific provisions of the bill on constitutional or other grounds.	48
Single-interest groups	Interest groups which represent a single interest (e.g. gun rights or pro-life issues).	105
Soft money	Money donated to political parties instead of to candidates to avoid campaign finance limitations. Parties are allowed to spend the money on certain campaigning activities (e.g. voter registration and get-out-the-vote drives).	84
Split-ticket voting	Voting for candidates of two or more parties for different offices at the same election (the opposite of straight-ticket voting).	91
Standing committee	A permanent, policy-specialist committee of Congress playing key roles in both legislation and investigation.	25
Stare decisis	A legal principle that judges should look to past precedents as a guide wherever possible (literally, 'let the decision stand').	61
Straight-ticket voting	Voting for candidates of the same party for different offices at the same election.	91
Strict constructionist	A Supreme Court justice who interprets the Constitution strictly or literally and tends to stress the retention of power by individual states.	58
Subpoena	A summons or demand for something.	29
Super PAC	A political committee that makes independent expenditures, but does not make contributions to candidates.	84
Super Tuesday	A Tuesday in February or early March when a number of states coincide their presidential primaries and caucuses to try to gain influence.	80
Supermajority	Where approval is required by a two-thirds majority of Congress.	11
Swing justice	The pivotal justice in an otherwise evenly balanced Court, who will often be in a position of casting the deciding vote.	58
Ultra vires	Latin phrase (literally, 'beyond the powers') used to describe an action that is beyond one's legal power or authority.	68
Unanimous consent	A legislative process whereby a legislator requests approval by all representatives to a rule change or law, without requiring a formal vote.	29
Unified government	When both houses of Congress and the presidency are controlled by the same party.	46